ENERGY
Where is God in it?

By

Jeremy Lopez

Energy: Where is God in it?

By Dr. Jeremy Lopez
Copyright © 2020

This book is licensed solely for your personal enjoyment only. This book may not be re-sold or given away to other people. If you would like to share this book with another person, please purchase an additional copy for each recipient. If you're reading this book and you did not purchase it or it was not purchased for your use only, please return to your favorite book retailer and purchase your own copy.

All rights reserved. This book is protected under the copyright laws of the United States of America. This book may not be copied or reprinted for commercial gain or profit. The use of short quotations or occasional page copying for personal or group study is permitted and encouraged.

Published by Identity Network
P.O. Box 38213
Birmingham, AL 35238
www.IdentityNetwork.net

ENDORSEMENTS

"You are put on this earth with incredible potential and a divine destiny. This powerful, practical man shows you how to tap into power you didn't even know you had." – Brian Tracy – Author, The Power of Self Confidence

"I found myself savoring the concepts of the Law of Attraction merging with the Law of Creativity until slowly the beautiful truths seeped deeper into my thirsty soul. I am called to be a Creator! My friend, Dr. Jeremy Lopez, has a way of reminding us of our eternal 'I-Am-ness' while putting the tools in our hands to unlock our endless creative

potential with the Divine mind. As a musical composer, I'm excited to explore, with greater understanding, the infinite realm of possibilities as I place fingers on my piano and whisper, 'Let there be!'" – Dony McGuire, Grammy Award winning artist and musical composer

"Jeremy dives deep into the power of consciousness and shows us that we can create a world where the champion within us can shine and how we can manifest our desires to live a life of fulfillment. A must read!" – Greg S. Reid – Forbes and Inc. top rated Keynote Speaker

*"I have been privileged to know Jeremy Lopez for many years, as well as sharing the platform with him at a number of conferences. Through this time, I have

found him as a man of integrity, commitment, wisdom, and one of the most networked people I have met. Jeremy is an entrepreneur and a leader of leaders. He has amazing insights into leadership competencies and values. He has a passion to ignite this latent potential within individuals and organizations and provide ongoing development and coaching to bring about competitive advantage and success. I would highly recommend him as a speaker, coach, mentor, and consultant." – Chris Gaborit – Learning Leader, Trainer

CONTENTS

Preface	p.1
Introduction	p.7
Illumination	p.31
The Energy of Faith	p.47
"The Effectual"	p.65
Energeo	p.81
Tangible Transfers	p.103
Infinite	p.129
The Spirit in Science	p.149
Frequency and Vibration	p.171
The Miraculous Mind	p.191
Mastery	p.203

DEDICATION

This book is dedicated to the seekers and to all who continue to ask questions in pursuit of a greater understanding of the things of God. To all who seek, the answers are given. To all who knock, doorways are opened. My prayer for you is that you would realize, truly, there is a power at work in you - a power which, like hope, springs eternal.

PREFACE

It's the most universal, most transcendent force there is. Without it, all life and all existence as we know it would instantly cease to be. This great, transcendent force which, according to science, comprises everything in the universe, is termed, simply, "energy." Without it, there would be no movement. There could be no life. Without it, even the matter of the physical world would instantaneously cease. But where is God in it all?

If you're reading this book, I would assume that, like me, you're a seeker who has never been afraid to ask questions. To even have a desire to read a book entitled *Energy: Where is God in it?* is proof-positive that you question things. In fact, I would dare to suggest that at times some have probably even called you a "trouble maker" for for the questions you've asked. To even begin to consider the role that God plays within something such as energy, to most, at first glance, would seem almost blasphemous or heretical. Some would consider such a question to be quite "New Age," in fact.

It's a question that I can't help but to ponder within my own life - a question that I continue to ask more and more each day. How does one even begin to attempt to define such a concept as energy? Words often fail us when attempting to define such an ethereal, somewhat abstract idea. Sure; there are the terms, the definitions, and the labels of science - terms that will be analyzed in great detail within the pages of this book. Yet, on an even greater, grander scale, to begin to define a concept such as energy is akin to one's attempt to define God. How does one define that which is truly undefinable? To define energy is akin to attempting to define Spirit.

It was Jesus who once likened the Spirit to the wind. It blows, and we know fully well of its existence. It's invisible, and yet we know it's there. We know this because we see the effects of it. The same is true of energy. And the same is true of God.

Rarely do I ever do this; however, I feel, in total transparency, you deserve a warning - a disclaimer, of sorts. The revelations contained within this book are not for the faint of heart. For the religious mind, this book may seem offensive. To the mindset that has no desire to change or to evolve into a greater measure of awakening, this book will cause great damage. Consider yourself warned. My prayer, though, is that the words contained within this book will not only obliterate the religious spirit of limitation from within the minds of all who read them, but that awakening would come in even greater measure than any offense. For the mind to become renewed, it must first be challenged. It must be stretched beyond it's comfort zone - stretched beyond the normality of complacency.

As you read these words, my humble prayer for you and for all who read them is that there would be birthed a greater hunger than ever before to not only see but to also experience the effects of God. Like energy, where God is concerned, you've heard all the terms before. You know the scriptures. You speak the language of religion perhaps so well that maybe your "Christianity" is like a second language to you. You have the form, and you have it very well. You've mastered it, in fact. But, I would ask, are you seeing the effects of the God you speak of? You may very well have the form of Godliness, but do you have the power?

INTRODUCTION

"The Force is what gives a Jedi his power. It's an energy field created by all living things. It surrounds us and penetrates us. It binds the galaxy together." Released worldwide on May 25, 1977, Star Wars immediately became a global phenomenon - which many consider a masterpiece even to this very day. The quote, spoken by Sir Alec Guinness in his role as the mystical Obi-Wan Kenobi, describes the otherworldly power wielded by Luke Skywalker in his quest

to save the galaxy from certain destruction. The sci-fi blockbuster was considered a long-shot at the time, though, and almost never came to be. Writer and creator George Lucas relied heavily upon metaphysical, spiritual concepts when creating the draft of the film - concepts such as good and evil, light and darkness, and metaphysical, ubiquitous concepts such as energy, which he termed "The Force.".

A concept such as the mysterious "Force" seemed so very new at the time - so otherworldly. But all throughout history, man has longed to better understand the invisible, intangible realm which operates behind the scenes within Creation. Throughout the ages, religions have risen and many diverse philosophies espoused in often rather futile attempts to better define the invisible realm - and to define *God*. Believe it or not, religions throughout the ages have had much to say about the topic of energy, and throughout the ages, many various philosophies and even the scientific and medical arts have attempted to better understand it. The beliefs regarding energy, though, have long-since been as diverse and as varied as the many philosophies and religions that have attempted to define it. Surprisingly, as you will soon realize, it's almost impossible to separate talk of energy from talk of faith and belief.

Although I'll say here at the very offset that it's impossible to define what in many ways is truly undefinable and that the nature of God transcends all of the many labels and terms we use to define God, terms, definitions, and beliefs matter greatly. The words we use to offer description to God matter - not because God needs our terms or our definitions but because our terms help to paint pictures by which we, ourselves, better understand our own beliefs. The concept of energy is such an otherworldly term. It's invisible. It's ethereal. It's non-corporeal. Yet, we know it exists - like God.

But if everything is energy, as science has confirmed over and over again throughout the ages, what does this fact have to do with matters of faith, where a belief in God is concerned? It can seem so very "New Age" to even consider the question, can't it? The very question offends and challenges the religious mindset. Let's face it, when was the last time you heard - or maybe even told someone that they shouldn't start a daily yoga practice because it opens the doorway to demons and to the occult? Where does such a belief come from? Do the scriptures even say such things, where energy is concerned? Or have we all too often just continued to espouse the beliefs we've been taught without ever really studying to show ourselves approved?

If even the human body is energy, are we responsible for maintaining our own energy levels? And if everything around us is energy, also, what does that even mean? Most of all, what are we to do with such knowledge? Are we to even ask about it? Or, like so many other things where religion is concerned, are we to just sweep it underneath the rug and accept what we've always been told?

I started asking questions a long, long time ago. Surprisingly, it didn't end

my faith; it only strengthened my faith. I often like to use this analogy where questioning is concerned - particularly where matters of faith are concerned: "If you truly love something, wouldn't you try to better understand it?" If you truly love someone, wouldn't you spend all the time you could attempting to get to know them better? Wouldn't you want to know what they like and dislike? All too often, though, where religion is concerned, we're told that certain things are off-limits. Usually, where organized religion is concerned, we're often told to "sit down" and "shut up."
What I know beyond the shadow of any doubt, though, is that not only is it alright to ask questions, but that the questions take us into the deeper, more hidden truths. It was Jesus, in fact, who said that all who ask will receive.

He went on to say that to all who knock, the doorway will become opened. You and I have a promise that the Holy Spirit will lead us into all truths. The journey toward truth, though, is often equally as painful a process of discovery as it is a journey of adventure. Sometimes you learn that what you've been told for so long has been incorrect. Sometimes you learn that your beliefs weren't serving you. Let's face it; sometimes it hurts to grow up.

When the Holy Spirit began to impress upon me the revelations contained within this book, I felt a tremendous weight of responsibility. It was overwhelming, in fact. Even as I write these words to you, I know fully well how challenging it can be to question one's beliefs. It can be painful, at times. The journey toward greater understanding and revelation can so often cause such an inner catharsis - a very real, inner shaking. When the pain ends, though, the road ahead becomes all the more clear in light of new discovery. For you, my friend and fellow seeker, I firmly, wholeheartedly believe that within the pages of this book, you're going to find not only a revelation that has never been shared before, but that you will experience a deeper realm of the miraculous and the supernatural within your own life and journey of faith. That is, if you'll become willing to change and to evolve in your beliefs.

Perhaps like you, my life has been consumed with my faith for as long as I can even remember. Even from a very early age, my mother and father told me about the goodness of God. My father dedicated his entire life to the Gospel and to loving people; he remains my greatest inspiration even to this day. Even at an early age, I became aware of my own prophetic gift, knowing in some way that the gift of prophecy would define most of my life. I had no way of knowing then, though, that I would one day have the honor of prophesying to heads of business, heads of state, world leaders and celebrities. I had no way of knowing how the prophetic gift would manifest. Suffice it to say, I believe wholeheartedly in a supernatural life, and that belief in the supernatural has helped to define my life.

The journey of faith is a journey of discovery - and it's never ending. The journey toward revelation always begins with asking questions. For me, all those years ago, I found myself consumed with questions - questions that, throughout the years, have led to bestselling books and countless opportunities to minister throughout the world. I don't ask questions because I question God; I ask questions because I love God. He's my passion. For me, I strongly believe that it's impossible to read and to study the scriptures and to delve into the rich history of the faith without asking questions. Truly, there's something to be said about asking, seeking, and knocking.

But - back to energy - what role does that serve within matters of faith? Is energy just something invisible that turns on the lights when a light switch is flipped? Is energy something that powers cars and fuels horsepower? Is energy just merely something that causes us to stand up and to walk - something that rests while we're sleeping and something that activates again in the morning when we awaken? You see, a better understanding of energy is not only important where daily life is concerned, but it's also important where the faith is concerned. When Paul spoke of there being a "power" which works in us, what, exactly, was he referring to? Was he speaking solely of some ethereal, invisible, non-corporeal thing or was he speaking so something much more tangible - physical, even?

I therefore, the prisoner of the Lord, beseech you that ye walk worthy of the vocation wherewith ye are called,

2 With all lowliness and meekness, with longsuffering, forbearing one another in love;

3 Endeavouring to keep the unity of the Spirit in the bond of peace.

4 There is one body, and one Spirit, even as ye are called in one hope of your calling;

5 One Lord, one faith, one baptism,

6 One God and Father of all, who is above all, and through all, and in you all.

7 But unto every one of us is given grace according to the measure of the gift of Christ.

8 Wherefore he saith, When he ascended up on high, he led captivity captive, and gave gifts unto men.

9 (Now that he ascended, what is it but that he also descended first into the lower parts of the earth?

10 He that descended is the same also that ascended up far above all heavens, that he might fill all things.)

11 And he gave some, apostles; and some, prophets; and some, evangelists; and some, pastors and teachers;

12 For the perfecting of the saints, for the work of the ministry, for the edifying of the body of Christ:

13 Till we all come in the unity of the faith, and of the knowledge of the Son of God, unto a perfect man, unto the measure of the stature of the fulness of Christ:

14 That we henceforth be no more children, tossed to and fro, and carried about with every wind of doctrine, by the sleight of men, and cunning craftiness, whereby they lie in wait to deceive;

15 But speaking the truth in love, may grow up into him in all things, which is the head, even Christ:

16 From whom the whole body fitly joined together and compacted by that which every joint supplieth, according to the effectual working in the measure of every part, maketh increase of the body unto the edifying of itself in love.

17 This I say therefore, and testify in the Lord, that ye henceforth walk not as other Gentiles walk, in the vanity of their mind,

18 Having the understanding darkened, being alienated from the life of God through the ignorance that is in them, because of the blindness of their heart:

19 Who being past feeling have given themselves over unto lasciviousness, to work all uncleanness with greediness.

20 But ye have not so learned Christ;

21 If so be that ye have heard him, and have been taught by him, as the truth is in Jesus:

22 That ye put off concerning the former conversation the old man, which is corrupt according to the deceitful lusts;

23 And be renewed in the spirit of your mind;

24 And that ye put on the new man, which after God is created in righteousness and true holiness.

25 Wherefore putting away lying, speak every man truth with his neighbour: for we are members one of another.

26 Be ye angry, and sin not: let not the sun go down upon your wrath:

27 Neither give place to the devil.

28 Let him that stole steal no more: but rather let him labour, working with his hands the thing which is good, that he may have to give to him that needeth.

29 Let no corrupt communication proceed out of your mouth, but that which is good to the use of edifying, that it may minister grace unto the hearers.

30 And grieve not the holy Spirit of God, whereby ye are sealed unto the day of redemption.

31 Let all bitterness, and wrath, and anger, and clamour, and evil speaking, be put away from you, with all malice:

32 And be ye kind one to another, tenderhearted, forgiving one another, even as God for Christ's sake hath forgiven you. (Ephesians 4:1-32 KJV)

In Paul's epistle to the early church at Corinth, he alludes to the nature of God as being a power that's "above all," "in all," and "working in all." Such a claim is very easy to be overlooked, when looked at through the lens of the natural, religious mind. It's so very easy to see such a claim and relate it, simply, to "God's in everything." If so, what does that truly mean? Could it be that even the ancients had a revelation concerning the mysterious power of energy, even in their days? Could it be that further unlocking the secret of those revelations could be the catalyst which fuels the miraculous and the supernatural? Furthermore, could it be that the true meaning of Paul's claims lay at the very heart of exactly why there was so much power at work in the early church?

For this cause I bow my knees unto the Father of our Lord Jesus Christ,

15 Of whom the whole family in heaven and earth is named,

16 That he would grant you, according to the riches of his glory, to be strengthened with might by his Spirit in the inner man;

17 That Christ may dwell in your hearts by faith; that ye, being rooted and grounded in love,

18 May be able to comprehend with all saints what is the breadth, and length, and depth, and height;

19 And to know the love of Christ, which passeth knowledge, that ye might be filled with all the fulness of God.

20 Now unto him that is able to do exceeding abundantly above all that we ask or think, according to the power that worketh in us, that some will never be able to taste and to see the goodness of God - that is, if it's true that Christ is working in all. Surely, the Christ within us all does a better job than that.

What I mean to say and why isn't the church seeing the effects of what it claims to believe? When Jesus spoke of the Holy Spirit, comparing Him to the wind, he noted that we can always know of the existence of something by being able to see the effects of it. We can't see the wind, but we know if its existence because we see the effects of it. We watch as trees begin to rustle. We see movement and even feel the cool breeze upon our skin. The wind is effective.

There's a power at work in you that for far too long hasn't been very effective. In fact, this power has been lying dormant for much longer than you may have realized. There's a reason that Paul admonished Timothy to stir up the gift that was within him. The reason, quite simply, is because the power within must be activated if it's ever to become effective. If you're tired of believing in miracles but never seeing the miraculous in your life or in your church, read on. If you're tired of hearing about the supernatural without ever truly witnessing the supernatural and living a supernatural life, read on. Yes; there's a power that's at work within you even now. It's time to activate it. It's time to turn the power back on.

CHAPTER ONE
ILLUMINATION

A while back, I wrote a book called *HEALING: Energy, the Bible, Science and You*. It's since been referred to as one of the most comprehensive books ever written on the topic of divine, spiritual healing. In it, I share the actual mechanics at work behind topics like faith healing, the Word of Faith movement, and the Law of Attraction, as those topics relate to physical healing. The book went on to become an international bestseller and is still, to this very day, one of our most requested products at Identity Network.

I have to admit that I was little shocked by the immense, global response.

When we think of topics like healing, where the journey of faith is concerned, we so often think of the concept of physical healing - particularly within the more Pentecostal, more charismatic circles of Christianity. In the pages of this book, I'll share even more on the topic of healing, as we delve into the great mysteries of energy and the role energy plays within the physical, human body. But I wanted to begin this journey into the topic of energy by sharing with you, first, just how important the concept of understanding truly is - particularly where faith is concerned. In order to even begin to delve into the concept of energy requires, first, an understanding that there's always, always more than meets the eye.

There's always so much more going on around us than what the natural, naked eye is able to discern and interpret. As we journey into what I truly feel is one of the most-needed revelations today, I want to begin by saying, first, that when Paul spoke of the dangers of being "ignorant" where spiritual gifts are concerned, he wasn't speaking merely of the gift of prophecy, the gift of healing, or the gift of diverse tongues in operation within the early church. He wasn't speaking solely of the many miracles, signs, and wonders that so consumed the early church - those signs and notable wonders which Jesus said would follow the lives of believers, according to the sixteenth chapter of the Gospel of Mark. He was speaking of something even deeper - even more innate and much more universal. He was speaking of a power at work within and all around all things.

It's so easy today, especially in this more modern world of ours, to think of the early church in a somewhat primitive way. It was so long ago, we think, surely they didn't understand concepts such as energy, metaphysics, frequency, and vibration. Surely, we so often think, they weren't as advanced as we are today. I often think this myself. However, what's truly shocking is that even in times and cultures predating even the rise of the early church, there were notable philosophers even within ancient Greece who devoted themselves to the study of the unseen, invisible realms. Even then, there was science and medicine - though, admittedly, crude by today's standards. However, what if the ancient world actually had a much better understanding of the power of energy than most believe? What if even the early church considered energy in its early writings and in the formation of beliefs that would become the central premise of the faith? In fact, what if energy has been a vital, integral part of the life of faith all along? And what if science only serves to confirm what the ancients knew all along?

It's of interesting note that even within the religion of Judaism and in the more mystical teachings of Kabbalah, the concept of energy is even considered paramount. What we all too often seem to forget in this more modern age of ours, where religion is concerned, is that the faith of Christianity has always had strong ties to the Jewish mystics. Were it not for the ancient prophets and seers of old within Jewish history, much of what we now refer to as the scriptures of the Holy Bible simply would not be. There were "modern marvels" all along - even in the stories of faith. It took precision and science to build pyramids. It took precision, even, to construct the wilderness tabernacle of Moses.

When the wilderness tabernacle of Moses was dedicated, the scriptures state that the glory of God was so strong and so forceful that neither Moses nor his brother Aaron could even stand under the heavy weight - the *chabod* - of the glory. There was literal "force" being exerted from within the glory. Jewish mystics of old also referred to this glory ass being "visible" and able to be seen with the natural, naked eye - the *Shekinah*. Some religious and historical scholars have even gone as far as to interpret certain texts from within the Talmud to mean that the Ark of the Covenant of God was actually able to float and to levitate. Though the priests were commanded to carry the Ark with poles made from Acacia wood, a certain term in the Hebrew writings alludes to the encounter at the crossing of the Jordan river in which the feet of the priests were actually "lifted up" to the dry land on the sides of the river bed. Some Jewish mystics even believe that the reason Uzzah was smitten by the Lord for helping to steady the Ark was not because he physically touched it, as religions have claimed, but because the Ark was capable of "carrying itself." This legend which would ultimately lead to much of what was seen in the popular film Raiders of the Lost Ark came not from Hollywood but from actual Jewish mythology. If the assertions of some of the early Jewish writers and historians are true, we aren't dealing simply with spiritual concepts but with very real, very tangible forces of energy - very powerful energies, in fact. What if there was an actual force of energy which healed not only the blinded eyes in the many marvelous accounts from Jesus' ministry, but what if it was, in fact, a very real, very tangible flow of energy at work within the woman's body as she touched the hem of his garment? If you look beyond the labels and the many terms of religion, what you find is that energy has been present within matters of faith all along. Understanding this, though, demands a certain sense of illumination.

Jesus believed wholeheartedly in the concept of energy; he termed it, simply "The Kingdom." When Paul would later write to the church at Ephesus regarding the power at work within all, he was merely quoting the words of Jesus himself. Furthermore, when Paul wrote to the church that had been established in Corinth, speaking of the spiritual gifts in operation, he was referencing not only the corporate, ecclesia of the Body of Christ; he was speaking even more so about a very real, very tangible energy at work within the human body itself. The "power" at work within us is the very real essence of the Kingdom which Jesus spoke of. It's an internal realm. It's the world within.

And when he was demanded of the Pharisees, when the kingdom of God should come, he answered them and said, The kingdom of God cometh not with observation:

21 Neither shall they say, Lo here! or, lo there! for, behold, the kingdom of God is within you.

22 And he said unto the disciples, The days will come, when ye shall desire to see one of the days of the Son of man, and ye shall not see it.

23 And they shall say to you, See here; or, see there: go not after them, nor follow them.

24 For as the lightning, that lighteneth out of the one part under heaven, shineth unto the other part under heaven; so shall also the Son of man be in his day.

25 But first must he suffer many things, and be rejected of this generation.

26 And as it was in the days of Noe, so shall it be also in the days of the Son of man.

27 They did eat, they drank, they married wives, they were given in marriage, until the day that Noah entered into the ark, and the flood came, and destroyed them all.

28 Likewise also as it was in the days of Lot; they did eat, they drank, they bought, they sold, they planted, they builded;

29 But the same day that Lot went out of Sodom it rained fire and brimstone from heaven, and destroyed them all.

30 Even thus shall it be in the day when the Son of man is revealed. (Luke 17:20-30 KJV)

When Paul spoke of the power that works in us, around us, and through us, he was denoting the words of Jesus - speaking of the Kingdom *within.* It's interesting to note, though, that Jesus was speaking not only to his disciples when he shared this truth regarding the realm of Heaven; he was speaking to the religious elite of his day, also - he was speaking of a very real, very internal realm that exists beyond the confines of belief and beyond the beliefs of certain creeds and dogma. He was speaking to nonbelievers also! This realm which Jesus spoke of is a universal, expansive realm - one permeating all things. The Kingdom of Heaven - the rule and reign of God - has always been much more universal than what most religions would dare to admit. What if He truly is LORD of all? What if He truly is the propitiation of our sins and, also, the sins of the whole world?

I share this, here at the very offset, to say, simply, what would happen if the church began to truly believe what it claims to believe? What if it truly, as never before, could gain the insight into the supremacy of the Kingdom of Heaven, being able to see that it truly encompasses all things and all people? Christendom, contrary to what we now see so prevalent in the modern age, was never intended to be so divisive. Today, with more than 33,000 various sects within Christianity, with each denomination having its own various beliefs, could it be that somewhere along the way we lost sight of the to experience the realm beyond. But when the eyes of understanding do become enlightened and when understanding does come, not only does the mind become able to perceive the invisible realms, but a very real connection is made to the inner power at work within. Like energy, God is the force at work behind all things - working above all, and through all, and in us all. Nowhere in existence is there a place where the glorious Presence of God is not known. As the psalmist declared, even if you were to make your bed in the very depths of Hell, still, there you would find Him. Nothing is beyond His Presence. And insomuch as nothing is beyond His Presence, nothing is beyond His mighty power - the same power at work in you.

CHAPTER TWO
THE ENERGY OF FAITH

For centuries, the concept of faith has been viewed in such a passive way. It's viewed, primarily, as little more than just belief and little or nothing more than that. "Just believe," we're told. "Just have faith." Unfortunately, the concept of faith has been relegated to little more than a cliche or religious mantra - a buzz word that has been used to excuse our moments of laziness and inactivity. Faith, though, has never been a passive term. Faith has always demanded action.

As I began to research the topic of faith for my book *Manifesting Your Prophetic Word*, what I came to realize early on is that the early church in no way regarded the concept of faith in the way that we do, now within the more modern era. To them, faith was always living and active. It was never passive. It was always present. It possessed its own force - its own energy unto itself.

Belief, in and of itself, has never truly been enough to lay claim to the abundant life. In fact, specifics and details matter where beliefs are concerned. I'm sure you've realized by now that, contrary to what religion has claimed for centuries, it actually is possible to believe all the wrong things - even when the belief is sincere. I mean to say that it's actually possible to be sincerely wrong. It's not only alright to admit when you're wrong; faith demands it. I assure you that the Holy Spirit already knows.

Could it be that for far too long the Body of Christ has viewed the term "faith" in all the wrong ways - as little more than just a mere belief? And could it be that this is the central, underlying reason why the effects of the Spirit aren't as prevalent as they once were in the beginning? Could it be that the reason the church seems to so often lack the power and the Presence it claims to have is because it has for centuries viewed faith in incorrect ways? What if we've believed all the wrong things about faith?

Is it enough to simply believe, as we've been taught? Is belief, itself, enough to manifest the intended, desired outcome? Or are specifics needed? If I believe

5 If any of you lack wisdom, let him ask of God, that giveth to all men liberally, and upbraideth not; and it shall be given him.

6 But let him ask in faith, nothing wavering. For he that wavereth is like a wave of the sea driven with the wind and tossed.

7 For let not that man think that he shall receive any thing of the Lord.

8 A double minded man is unstable in all his ways.

9 Let the brother of low degree rejoice in that he is exalted:

10 But the rich, in that he is made low: because as the flower of the grass he shall pass away.

11 For the sun is no sooner risen with a burning heat, but it withereth the grass, and the flower thereof falleth, and the grace of the fashion of it perisheth: so also shall the rich man fade away in his ways.

12 Blessed is the man that endureth temptation: for when he is tried, he shall receive the crown of life, which the Lord hath promised to them that love him.

13 Let no man say when he is tempted, I am tempted of God: for God cannot be tempted with evil, neither tempteth he any man:

14 But every man is tempted, when he is drawn away of his own lust, and enticed.

15 Then when lust hath conceived, it bringeth forth sin: and sin, when it is finished, bringeth forth death.

16 Do not err, my beloved brethren.

17 Every good gift and every perfect gift is from above, and cometh down from the Father of lights, with whom is no variableness, neither shadow of turning.

18 Of his own will begat he us with the word of truth, that we should be a kind of firstfruits of his creatures.

19 Wherefore, my beloved brethren, let every man be swift to hear, slow to speak, slow to wrath:

20 For the wrath of man worketh not the righteousness of God.

21 Wherefore lay apart all filthiness and superfluity of naughtiness, and receive with meekness the engrafted word, which is able to save your souls.

22 But be ye doers of the word, and not hearers only, deceiving your own selves.

23 For if any be a hearer of the word, and not a doer, he is like unto a man beholding his natural face in a glass:

24 For he beholdeth himself, and goeth his way, and straightway forgetteth what manner of man he was.

25 But whoso looketh into the perfect law of liberty, and continueth therein, he

8 Finally, brethren, whatsoever things are true, whatsoever things are honest, whatsoever things are just, whatsoever things are pure, whatsoever things are lovely, whatsoever things are of good report; if there be any virtue, and if there be any praise, think on these things.

9 Those things, which ye have both learned, and received, and heard, and seen in me, do: and the God of peace shall be with you. (Philippians 4:5-9 KJV)

In Paul's writing to the church, he stresses the need for doing, noting the early believers were to enact and to do the things they had seen him do. But what had they seen? What were the things they had witnessed him doing? Merely proclaiming the Gospel and recruiting others to join the cause of Christ? Or had they seen something more?

And I, brethren, when I came to you, came not with excellency of speech or of wisdom, declaring unto you the testimony of God.

2 For I determined not to know any thing among you, save Jesus Christ, and him crucified.

3 And I was with you in weakness, and in fear, and in much trembling.

4 And my speech and my preaching was not with enticing words of man's wisdom, but in demonstration of the Spirit and of power:

5 That your faith should not stand in the wisdom of men, but in the power of God.

6 Howbeit we speak wisdom among them that are perfect: yet not the wisdom of this world, nor of the princes of this world, that come to nought:

7 But we speak the wisdom of God in a mystery, even the hidden wisdom, which God ordained before the world unto our glory:

8 Which none of the princes of this world knew: for had they known it, they would not have crucified the Lord of glory.

9 But as it is written, Eye hath not seen, nor ear heard, neither have entered into the heart of man, the things which God hath prepared for them that love him.

10 But God hath revealed them unto us by his Spirit: for the Spirit searcheth all things, yea, the deep things of God. (1 Corinthians 2:1-10 KJV)

In the life and ministry of Paul, there was a demonstration of the "power." The power wasn't merely spoken of but was literally evidenced through action and through works. According to the scriptures as recounted in Acts, God wrought "special" miracles through the hands of Paul. There's truly something to be said about the power of action - about putting action to the belief. It's not enough, you see, to simply believe in powerful things. It's time to begin to do powerful things. And if the powerful things are never accomplished - or can't be done - then its an indicator that you either do not believe what you claim to believe or that you're believing moment of timing - all the energy of Creation became enacted the moment the lame man got up. You see, the supernatural and the miraculous can only be enacted when you put action to your faith. As you will see, energy and action have always been central to the Gospel all along. The secret that religion doesn't want you to know is that even in the early church, they were aware of the power of energy and of movement. The entire Kingdom, in fact, exists on the basis of energy. Without action, there is no manifestation. And, as the scriptures remind us, without works, there is truly is no faith at all.

CHAPTER THREE
"THE EFFECTUAL"

It was in the foothills of the Appalachian mountains in the latter part of the nineteenth century when a group of seekers began to study the Book of Acts. It was 1886 and the location was Barney Creek. Like you, these believers had grown tired and weary of the status quo of religion. Like you, they wanted more. At the time, it was uncommon, almost unheard of, to practice speaking in tongues. It was a common belief that the gifts had ceased in operation - ending with the death of the last Apostle. The common belief at the time - and the belief permeating centuries before - was that the supernatural existed solely for a specific time and for a select dispensation, to bring about the Apostolic Age.

Pentecost had never truly ended, though. The gifts had never truly ceased. They were simply no longer believed in by most Protestant believers at the time. It was this time of resurgence that would give rise to what we now refer to as the charismatic movement of the faith. In the coming decades, pioneers such as William Branham, Aimee Semple McPherson, Kathryn Kuhlman, and Oral Roberts would bring a message of divine healing to the world, bringing a renewed sense of fervor to better know what Kuhlman would come to term "the person of the Holy Spirit." There would have been no Azusa Street revival were it not for those early believers questioning the status quo of the day. There would be no talk of miracles, signs, and wonders. Chances are you and I wouldn't even have a passion for the realm of God were it not for those believers refusing to settle for the traditions of the day.

The resurgence didn't come without great cost, though. There was persecution, even in 1886. The homes of the believers were burned to the ground - their doctrines labeled as "heresy" or as "witchcraft." Could the gifts find their place in the modern era of the church? Only time would tell.

With the renewed fervor for the Holy Spirit, though, came also great emphasis on the supernatural manifestations - manifestations such as laying hands on with you two truths. First, you will be given exactly what you believe, just as Jesus said. Secondly, when it comes to belief and faith, we're dealing not with some abstract concept but, rather, with a very real "energy."

When Jesus in the sixteenth chapter of the Gospel of Mark speaks of signs following after believers, what he was emphatically saying was that there would always be "effects" of beliefs. He was saying that all belief would, itself, create some lasting, real, visible effect - a very noticeable effect, in fact. Acts records that Simon was able to *see* that through the laying on of the apostles' hands the gift of the Holy Ghost was given. What exactly did he see? Jesus told those who looked on that if they wouldn't believe him for the words that he spoke to them then to believe him, instead, for the works that he did - for what they were able to *see*. In other words, even Jesus remarked the importance of beliefs being able to be seen and evidenced. But what, exactly, does this have to do with energy? Quite literally everything.

In Paul's epistle to the church at Corinth, in 1 Corinthians 12:6, the NASB version states that there are *varieties of effects*, but the same God who works all things in all persons. The term in the original Greek is *Energeo*, literally translated as "energy." In 1 Corinthians 12:10, when Paul speaks of of the diversity of the gifts, he states that to some there is the "effecting of miracles;" the term, again, is *Energeo* - meaning "energy." And in verse 11 of that same text, when Paul writes that there is one singular Spirit who works all these things, distributing to each one individually as He wills, the term is *Energeo*.

The concept of energy doesn't simply relate to the gifts, though. When Paul makes mention of the wide, "effective" doors for ministry that have been opened before him in 1 Corinthians 16:9, the term is *Energeo*. In 2 Corinthians 1:6, when Paul makes mention of the afflictions and sufferings of life being "effective," the term is *Energeo*, meaning "energy." And so what are we to make of this remarkable truth? Does such a truth not only radically shift the way in which we view the belief of the early church but also the way that we view the concept of faith? When the scriptures speak of the "effectual, fervent prayers" of the righteous availing much, the term, again, is *Energeo*, meaning "energy."

All throughout the entirety of the scriptures, we find a very real principle of "cause" and "effect" - a principle upon which much of the early tenets of the faith of Christianity was founded. The cause is the belief one holds, and the effect is the energy that is released as a result of that belief. There's a reason that Jesus spoke so often of the power of belief, noting that if we believe and not doubt that to us nothing shall be impossible. Your beliefs have always been effective. The question, simply, is are your beliefs having the desired, intended effect you wish to see? If not, it's time to change your belief.

What I've realized within my own life and throughout years of ministry, particularly in success coaching, is that regardless of how effective one is, there's always room to become much more effective. Effectiveness can always be increased. There can always be greater results gained and even greater effects caused. The cause of all effect, though, is the belief one holds. The early church and Jesus himself recognized this powerful principle. This principle, in fact, is Divine Law, established from even before the very beginning. As a man thinketh in his heart, so is he.

Yes; we know that life is the result of belief and thought. However, what we find all throughout the entirety of the sacred text of the scriptures is that there's a reason our thoughts manifest. The ancients and even the early church seemed to know and to recognize that our thoughts and beliefs emanate very real energy - that our thoughts and beliefs literally "energize" Creation around us, causing Creation to align in accordance with what we will.

As you can see, there is a very real "energy" - a very real "force" at work within our faith, causing our beliefs to literally take effect. As you will soon see and realize, though, even the beliefs we hold possess the energy of creative power. All throughout life, as you go about your day to day activities - even when you're having dinner and even while you sleep and even dream - your beliefs are resonating within you and all around you the very real energy of the Kingdom, causing very real "effects." Suffice it to say, your beliefs have always been effective; they've always been creating something for you. The disconnect, though, is that for far too long, most have failed to recognize that principle of cause and effect. Belief, being the cause and the manifestation of those beliefs being the effect, it can often be so very easy to confuse the two. When was the last time you looked at life and said to yourself, "This must be the will of God?"

You see, all too often, because of the disconnect of religion, rather than viewing the principle of cause and effect in the correct way, we look to life without ever really giving attention to the beliefs we hold, believing that if it's happening then surely it must be in accordance with God's perfect will. The principle of cause and effect, though, doesn't work that way - particularly where the realm of the Kingdom is concerned. In the realm of God, it's the belief that creates the effect. It's the belief that creates the energy to create and to attract.

And Peter calling to remembrance saith unto him, Master, behold, the fig tree which thou cursedst is withered away.

22 And Jesus answering saith unto them, Have faith in God.

23 For verily I say unto you, That whosoever shall say unto this mountain, Be thou removed, and be thou cast into the sea; and shall not doubt in his heart, but shall believe that those things which he saith shall come to pass; he shall have whatsoever he saith.

24 Therefore I say unto you, What things soever ye desire, when ye pray, believe that ye receive them, and ye shall have them.

25 And when ye stand praying, forgive, if ye have ought against any: that your Father also which is in heaven may forgive you your trespasses.

26 But if ye do not forgive, neither will your Father which is in heaven forgive your trespasses.

27 And they come again to Jerusalem: and as he was walking in the temple, there come to him the chief priests, and the scribes, and the elders,

28 And say unto him, By what authority doest thou these things? and who gave thee this authority to do these things?

29 And Jesus answered and said unto them, I will also ask of you one question, and answer me, and I will tell you by what authority I do these things. (Mark 11:21-29 KJV)

You've always had much more authority than you've realized. You've always been effective with your thoughts and beliefs. If you aren't experiencing the life of fulfillment and abundance, though, the reason isn't that you lack in effectiveness; the reason is that you believe the wrong things about God and about your own life. You're now seeing the effects of every belief you hold to, and the life that you now see as you look to your natural, daily life, is the direct result of the very real energy of Creation that you've enacted. As I shared within my book *The Universe is at Your Command: Vibrating the Creative Side of God*, literally all of Heaven and earth move to bring to pass the decrees and the commands you give

- according to your belief.

CHAPTER FOUR
ENERGEO

Your thoughts are working. Your belief is working. They are effective in manifesting, and with every passing thought, you are harnessing very real, very tangible energies within yourself and within the world around you to bring to pass all that you believe. In writing this book to you, my prayer is that not only would your faith come alive as never before but that you would begin to see, truly, just how powerful the energy of your belief has always been. You're being given exactly what you believe.

Your belief has always been working to manifest - even when you create a life that doesn't feel good.

It was decades ago, now, when the Holy Spirit first began to awaken my mind to the truth about the Law of Attraction, reminding me that we have the power of the Kingdom within us to manifest the abundant life. Since that time, I've been keenly aware of energy - realizing that energy is vital to all we do and that it correlates to what we think. I have to admit, though, that when the Holy Spirit began to share with me the revelation contained within the pages of this book, what I saw was truly remarkable. Not only is there a very real energy at work where our beliefs are concerned, bringing into effect the beliefs we hold, but, even more so, that energy of creative power is always at work. That energy never really ceases.

You know, now, that energy all throughout the scriptures is tied to the concept of effectiveness - cause and effect, in a very real way. However, to begin to have an even greater, even more comprehensive understanding of what this truly means where the power of God is concerned, it's important to look to the words of Jesus himself. In order to gain better insight, though, it's important to bear in mind the rich history of the language behind the sacred text of the scriptures. As I've said before, it's important that we study to show ourselves approved, not only reading the text but correctly discerning it, according to the origin of its language.

Jesus didn't speak the English language, to the shock and disbelief of some. He spoke a dialect of Aramaic. Contrary to the teachings of some historians and theologians, the entire language of the scriptures was, originally, Aramaic. It's a misnomer to simply say that the Old Testament was written entirely in Hebrew and the New Testament in Greek. The truth of the matter is that it's actually much more nuanced than that and it isn't as black and white as most would like to believe.

After the time in Jewish history noted as the Babylonian exile, there was an amalgamation of different, various cultures which influenced the Hebrew people, resulting in the language known as Aramaic - the language of Jesus and his disciples. However, as of the time of the ministry of Jesus, the ancient world was Romanized, the dominant influence of the time being Greek. And so, when the writings that would ultimately come to be canonized as the text of the Holy Bible were written within the first three centuries, the influence was Greek. This is why it's important to understand the text of the New Testament writings from the perspective of Greek - particularly Koine Greek - while, at the same time, maintaining discernment of the influence of Judaism in the writings. Christianity emerged at a time when Judaism was the religion of the day for Israel - which is why Jesus spoke of the Law and the prophets.

And so, bearing this great, rich history of the faith in mind, when we read concepts such as "energy," works", and even "power," we're given even greater revelation as to the intention of the early writers as they made use of these terms.

The Greek language is, itself, quite diverse. The Septuagint became the very first Greek translation of the original Hebrew Bible, later transcribed into Latin before arriving in the king's English. Language changes; it evolves. Is that to imply that the scriptures are errant and somehow not divinely inspired? Certainly not. That is to say, though, that history matters. Language matters. The words of the written "Word" matter.

If you were to search "What does the Bible say about energy healing?" you'd find some very frightening responses. Most of these responses from very well-intentioned, very sincere believers will mention things like "witchcraft," "New-Age," or the "occult." A popular search of the topic yields this answer from the ever-popular site

GotQuestions.org - a site devoted to answering questions about the Bible: *In a world where people are constantly grasping for deeper meaning, deeper spirituality, and a higher purpose, energy healing is one more New Age philosophy that presents itself as very desirable to human beings. Born with sin, we all come into the world with the strong belief that we are the center of the universe—that we are in control of our health, our bodies, our lives, our circumstances, and our destinies. Those who have not turned to God for Truth have no choice but to search for it within themselves.*

The practice of energy healing is not in itself a religion, but it is a pathway to one's own spirituality. It leads us on a personal journey that encourages us to focus on ourselves and how our energy is in synch with the energies of the cosmos, the earth, and all other life. Through this, we can supposedly be taught to heal ourselves by using clairvoyance to "visualize" where the negative energy is in order to determine the cause of the problem, whether it is physical, emotional or spiritual.

Reiki, a widely used energy healing technique, was said to have been developed by a Buddhist monk who used cosmic symbols for healing. Reiki claims to work by removing obstructions to the flow of life force energy throughout the body. These obstructions are allegedly caused by negative thoughts, actions, or feelings, which some believe are the fundamental cause of illness. Many even claim that employing this method is the way Jesus obtained His healing power, rather than attributing His power to the fact that He is God.

The use of energy healing encourages us to put our full trust in ourselves and our own bodies, which is a form of worship. For most who participate in energy healing, no recognition is given to the one true God, nor does He receive any praise for healing. The person using these methods of healing has made himself into his own god. Getting involved in energy healing is spiritually dangerous, to say the least.

The Bible tells us that Jesus is the One who came to heal. "Then Jesus said, 'Come to me, all of you who are weary and carry heavy burdens, and I will give you rest'" (Matthew 11:28). God does not want or expect us to help ourselves. He is the source of life, of all that is good and true. Those who refuse to acknowledge Jesus will never come to a place of spiritual healing. "For this people's heart has become calloused; they hardly hear with their ears, and they have closed their eyes. Otherwise they might see with their eyes, hear with their ears, understand with their hearts and turn, and I would heal them" (Matthew 13:15).

Notice the quote, "Getting involved in energy healing in spiritually dangerous, to say the least." It's said in such a matter-of-fact way. There's no discussion - no deeper analysis. It's one of many, many countless millions of examples in which religion, when it has no knowledge, simply seems to say, "Don't you dare even ask a question like that!" It's no wonder Paul stressed, even in his days, the dangers of being ignorant where spiritual gifts are concerned. Ignorance, in fact, is the thing Paul did warn against - not a study of "energy" in matters of faith. If you were to do online searches asking what the Bible says about things like yoga and meditation, you'll find very similar "scripted" responses.

As uncomfortable as it makes religion to admit, the "truth" isn't all that simple, though. When Paul speaks of spiritual gifts in the church, mentioning that the Spirit "works" all in all, the term in the original Greek is literally "energy." And this is even a reference, in many ways, to even the words of Jesus himself when he said his purpose was to "work the works of Him that sent him," in John chapter six. Wherever there is the work of the Kingdom, there is very real energy involved. Wherever there is belief and thought, there is the creative force of energetic flow. When critics say that I sound "New Age" when I teach things like Law of Attraction and Law of Creation, I humbly respond that we are in a literal, new age - the Age of the Kingdom.

The term *Energeo* is used a total of 25 times in the Bible, and variations of the Greek term are used even more repeatedly. *Energes* is used 3 times, *energema* is used twice, and *energeia* a total of 10 times, respectively. *Thayer's Greek Dictionary* defines the term *Energeo*, "To put forth power, to work for one, to aid one, to effect." *The Kittle Theological Dictionary of the New Testament* defines the term as "active energy." Understanding this not only sheds light into what the early writers intended, but helps to enlighten the journey of faith.

Looking at the scriptures in this light, through the lens of the original text, we find it confirmed even more than before the power of cause and effect where faith is concerned - that faith and belief are literally creating real effects through very real energies. At the heart of every miracle, there is energy. At the heart of every thought and every step of faith, there is energy. And, yet, this energy is always, always creating some very real effect in your life, even when you aren't always aware of it.

Energeo refers to energy "in action" or the overall "effects" of energy and is not to be confused with "the power" itself. When Jesus spoke of the "power" that would come upon the disciples as they tarried in Jerusalem, the term is *dunamis*, literally translated "power." When Paul speaks of the "power" at work within us, the term, again, is *dunamis*. The "work" of the power he mentions, though, is *energeo*, relating to the power's overall effectiveness within us. It's clear within the text that there is a very real, albeit subtle distinction between the two.

And so what are we to make of this difference in terminology? Was it merely a matter of semantics, or did it mean something much more? Does it give to us a greater glimpse of the truth regarding this matchless, inner power working within us? The question must be asked, what did the early church truly believe about the "power" of God? Understanding this in a more enlightened, more thorough way would not only serve to edify the faith but to also create more of an atmosphere for the miraculous even today.

It's clear in the writings, given the usage of the term *energeo* as separate from *dunami*s and Paul's emphatic statement of the power working in all, that the early church believed the power of God to be a universal and innate force - a force that, albeit is always present and always working, is not always as effective as other times. This statement, perhaps baffling to the natural, religious mind, seems almost blasphemous, at first glance. How could one even dare to make such a claim? Doesn't the power of God always work, without question? Yes and no.

Though the power is always working - though the power is always flowing - there are times when the power isn't "effective." There are times when it doesn't have the intended, desired result. We see this even in the earthly, physical life and ministry of Jesus himself. It's stated that at times he could do no mighty works because of unbelief - and that the religious traditions of man had made the Word of God to no "effect." Notice, again, the usage of the term "effect" - *energeo* and not *dunamis*. We find this in Mark. *Making the word of God of none effect through your tradition, which ye have dewlivered: and many such things like ye do. (Mark 7:13 KJV)* And so, is the power of God always flowing? Yes; however, the effectiveness on the power rests solely in the belief of the believer.

We find this confirmed even more in two specific accounts of notable miracles in Jesus' ministry - the raising of Jairus' daughter from the dead and also the healing of the woman with the issue of blood. In the account of the miraculous raising to life of the daughter of Jairus, we find that the atmosphere was first made conducive before the miracle ever took place - Jesus clearing the room of unbelievers. And in the account of the healing of the woman with the issue of blood, we find the account depicted in two ways within the Gospel records - one account going as far as to depict the work of the miracle being an inner work, as the woman said "within herself" that a miracle would take place before ever even touching the hem of Jesus' garment. Here we find a glimpse into what truly makes the energy of God become effective.

And a certain woman, which had an issue of blood twelve years,

26 And had suffered many things of many physicians, and had spent all that she had, and was nothing bettered, but rather grew worse,

27 When she had heard of Jesus, came in the press behind, and touched his garment.

28 For she said, If I may touch but his clothes, I shall be whole.

29 And straightway the fountain of her blood was dried up; and she felt in her body that she was healed of that plague.

30 And Jesus, immediately knowing in himself that virtue had gone out of him, turned him about in the press, and said, Who touched my clothes?

31 And his disciples said unto him, Thou seest the multitude thronging thee, and sayest thou, Who touched me?

32 And he looked round about to see her that had done this thing.

33 But the woman fearing and trembling, knowing what was done in her, came and fell down before him, and told him all the truth.

34 And he said unto her, Daughter, thy faith hath made thee whole; go in peace, and be whole of thy plague. (Mark 5:25-34 KJV)
And a woman having an issue of blood twelve years, which had spent all her living upon physicians, neither could be healed of any,

44 Came behind him, and touched the border of his garment: and immediately her issue of blood stanched.

45 And Jesus said, Who touched me? When all denied, Peter and they that were with him said, Master, the multitude throng thee and press thee, and sayest thou, Who touched me?

46 And Jesus said, Somebody hath touched me: for I perceive that virtue is gone out of me.

47 And when the woman saw that she was not hid, she came trembling, and falling down before him, she declared unto him before all the people for what cause she had touched him, and how she was healed immediately.

48 And he said unto her, Daughter, be of good comfort: thy faith hath made thee whole; go in peace. (Luke 8:43-48 KJV)

Within the depiction, we see the "effectiveness" of the energy being entirely dependent upon the actions of the woman - not dependent upon Jesus. In fact, as the accounts are recorded in both Gospels, Jesus is depicted as being almost oblivious to his surroundings, not recognizing a healing had even taken place until he sensed it. Was there always power present to heal? Was the power of God present and fully capable to bring the healing about? Yes; however, the power was only made "effective" in accordance with the belief of the woman. As you will soon see even more so, the energy of God is directly linked to the belief one holds to. It's the thoughts of man that enact the power of God. Such has always been the case.

CHAPTER FIVE
TANGIBLE TRANSFERS

The charismatic and Pentecostal movements within Christianity have long-since been questioned by those who believe the gifts ceased. Often times, many of these questions have been valid and warranted. As I've said before, the prophetic movement should always be tested. The scriptures, in fact, speak of this testing, admonishing that we try the spirits to see if they be of God. Throughout the history of the faith, there have always been moments of transition as new revelations have emerged, causing great paradigm shifts - revelations of healing, prophecy, and the miraculous.

There have always, though, been those moments of what I like to call tangible transference. These moments of tangible transfer - these moments of impartation - are are not only integral to the faith but are, even more so, integral to life itself. The tangible transfers of energy have always been part of one's daily life, regardless of the faith one holds. Miracles have never been relegated solely to the Christian faith. Man-made religion would love nothing more than to copyright and to patent the moving of the energy of God. God, however, cannot be contained. The realm of God transcends the labels and the definitions that we place upon it.

When we think of topics such as revival and outpouring, we think of the many times throughout history when the miraculous power of God was so evident - times when humanity found itself caught in the throes of those literal paradigm moments. Within the faith, we think to times and to seasons of awakening - times in which the fervor for the things of the Spirit were unmistakable and undeniable. Within the Pentecostal and charismatic circles of Christianity, we find these times of refreshing all the more. We find times, all throughout the great, rich history of the faith in which the charismata - the "gifts" - were so pronounced.

In these moments of transition within the faith, the power - the *dunamis* - was so present and so real; however, the effectiveness - the *energeo* - of that power was equally as present. Miracles happened. Signs followed. The preaching of the Gospel was confirmed through moments that could only be described as miraculous. And through it all, faith was refreshed.

I felt inspired by the Holy Spirit to include this chapter within the book to address what is truly a certain misunderstanding within the faith, regarding the movement of the Holy Spirit. When I first began to feel the inspiration and the revelation that would come to be the basis of this book, *Energy: Where is God in it?* I couldn't help but feel such a passionate hunger to say, "everywhere." He is above all, in all, through all, working all in all according to the good pleasure of His own will. And, as the psalmist wrote, there is literally nowhere in existence where the Presence of God is not known. All too often, though, where matters of faith are concerned - particularly with the topic of the miraculous - there seems to be this misnomer within the faith that suggests miracles, signs, and wonders are confined solely to the church and to the faith of Christianity. It simply isn't true.

Organized religion has no patent or copyright on the move of God. The Spirit cannot be contained and is constantly, always working throughout all faiths to lead all men toward revelation and understanding. Even as I write these words to you, I find myself reminded of those moments when I first received the revelation for my book *Healing: Energy, the bible, Science, and You*. As you now realize, there is a very real, very tangible force at work behind the scenes in all of Creation. This transcendent, divine force is integral to all existence and is the power which Paul spoke of when speaking even of the spiritual gifts in his letters to the church at Corinth.

In *Healing: Energy, the Bible, science, and You*, I share how the early church viewed the power at work within not only the Body of Christ as a whole but also within the human body itself. You are a carrier of energy - a vessel of the energies of Creation. This is the power working in you - a very real, very literal force capable of manifesting and bringing into the fabric of three-dimensional space and time all your desires according to your very own thoughts. Within the book, I share how thought is intrinsically interlinked to the manifestations of the miraculous.

When Paul writes of a "treasure" being within "earthen vessels," he's addressing, specifically, this inner, divine power.

Now there are diversities of gifts, but the same Spirit.

5 And there are differences of administrations, but the same Lord.

6 And there are diversities of operations, but it is the same God which worketh all in all.

7 But the manifestation of the Spirit is given to every man to profit withal.

8 For to one is given by the Spirit the word of wisdom; to another the word of knowledge by the same Spirit;

9 To another faith by the same Spirit; to another the gifts of healing by the same Spirit;

10 To another the working of miracles; to another prophecy; to another discerning of spirits; to another divers kinds of tongues; to another the interpretation of tongues:

11 But all these worketh that one and the selfsame Spirit, dividing to every man severally as he will.

12 For as the body is one, and hath many members, and all the members of that one body, being many, are one body: so also is Christ.

13 For by one Spirit are we all baptized into one body, whether we be Jews or

Gentiles, whether we be bond or free; and have been all made to drink into one Spirit.

14 For the body is not one member, but many.

15 If the foot shall say, Because I am not the hand, I am not of the body; is it therefore not of the body?

16 And if the ear shall say, Because I am not the eye, I am not of the body; is it therefore not of the body?

17 If the whole body were an eye, where were the hearing? If the whole were hearing, where were the smelling?

18 But now hath God set the members every one of them in the body, as it hath pleased him.

19 And if they were all one member, where were the body?

20 But now are they many members, yet but one body.

21 And the eye cannot say unto the hand, I have no need of thee: nor again the head to the feet, I have no need of you.

22 Nay, much more those members of the body, which seem to be more feeble, are necessary:

23 And those members of the body, which we think to be less honourable, upon these we bestow more abundant honour; and our uncomely parts have more abundant comeliness.

24 For our comely parts have no need: but God hath tempered the body together, having given more abundant honour to that part which lacked.

25 That there should be no schism in the body; but that the members should have the same care one for another. (1 Corinthians 12:4-25 KJV)

In the book, *Healing: Energy, the Bible, Science, and You*, I pose the question, what if Paul was speaking not only of the Body of Christ - the corporate body of believers - but was, in fact, also alluding to the physical, human body itself? Such a claim may seem quite shocking to the religious, natural mind - the mind which seems to think everyone believes the same things and holds to the same beliefs. Within the writings of Paul, we find an illustration of diversity - a picture of uniqueness and individuality. Yet, through it all, we also find a commonality, of sorts, and a sense of some universal bond working in all things. In the text, the term *energeo* refers to the Spirit "working" in all the "gifts." This direct reference to "energy" within the body cannot logically be speaking only of the corporate Body of Believers. If so, why would Paul feel it necessary to stress such individuality and uniqueness, noting that everyone operates differently? By painting this picture, Paul was speaking of something much, much more innate and much more universal than modern organized religion has claimed. He was speaking of a universal energy contained within the body itself - using it as an illustration to depict the working of the supernatural gifts within the corporate Body of Christ.

You are a carrier of the energy of Creation. And whether you realize it or not, this force of Creation has always been working within you and will continue to. The effectiveness of this power, though, is dependent not upon God but upon your very own thoughts and beliefs. After all, as Jesus said, we're given exactly what we believe. And, as the writer of the Gospel of Mark states, signs follow after belief.

What if I were to tell you that long before the teachings of Jesus were transformed by political forces to become the religion of Christianity and long before there was ever even a term

"Christian," even then there were miracles, signs, and wonders? What if I were to tell you that miracles existed long before the Day of Pentecost ever came? Bear in mind, even according to the text of the scriptures, the disciples were performing miracles long before even the crucifixion of Jesus - and they returned marveling that even demonic forces obeyed their commands. There was no Holy Bible. There had not even been a glorious Resurrection at the time. The disciples, even then, had learned to harness the creative force - the "Kingdom" - within them, realizing that, as Jesus had taught them, it was heir belief that made the power come alive and take "effect." This alludes to the energy of creative power being much, much more universal and much more expansive than modern religion would seem to suggest. This expanded power - this unlimited nature - seems to point toward a greater, more innate power residing within all and not just a select few. Could it be that the Glory of the LORD truly is in and around all things? Could it be that religion has never truly been able to define the realm of God and that the realm of the miraculous has always been within all men, just as Jesus said?

Today, particularly within the more modern lens of religion, when we think of the supernatural signs of the Spirit, we think primarily of those things listed within the sixteenth chapter of the Gospel of Mark and the gifts outlined within Paul's letters to the church at Corinth. We think of speaking in tongues, prophesy, and the healing of the sick through the laying on of hands.

It's most notably the laying on of hands that seems to so often be the focus. But did you know that many various other world religions have long regarded the healing of the sick and the laying on of hands, also? The concept is not primarily a Christian concept.

Many would find it shocking to know that for even centuries predating the rise of Christianity, in the east, in many various Hindu religions, notable gurus practiced "impartation" and "activation" through the laying on of hands. This is common even today through what is known as "shaktipat" - the laying on of hands and an exchange of "energy" between a mentor and a disciple, when a disciple chooses to follow a certain path. All through ancient sanskrit writings, we find that in the east, for centuries, there have always been the archetypes of the student-teacher model, with disciples wanting an impartation of the knowledge of the teacher. Oddly enough in the east, in moments of "shaktipat," there are common manifestations of supernatural, otherworldly occurrences that would rival even those found within the more Pentecostal, more charismatic circles within the Christian faith - with individuals speaking in tongues, being "slain in the Spirit," prophesying, and even having visions and entering into trance-like states similar to Peter on the rooftop of Cornelius.

Even within the Buddhist tradition, a great emphasis is placed upon mental, emotional, and physical healing. And within modern Spiritualism the ever-popular healing circles of the Victorian era are still all too common. It seems, too, that here in the west, there is a renewed interest in all the healing modalities, with concepts such as "energy" healing," reiki, and even the concept of "tapping" becoming more popular each year. I share much more about these healing modalities within my book *Healing: Energy, the Bible, Science, and You.* Suffice it to say, though, the "energy" working within the human body is a universal force - a force referred to in Asian cultures as "chi" - or "life force." When viewed through the lens of the natural, religious mind, these terms and concepts can seem quite mysterious or often be labeled as "New Age." Yet, with a better understanding of Paul's perspective concerning the spiritual gifts, it becomes clear that what the early church practiced following the Day of Pentecost wasn't altogether that different.

Today, if someone receives healing in a yoga studio, through the energy healing of reiki, or even through the practice of "tapping," the religious mind is quick to say, "That isn't of God." Yet, when someone is touched within a church setting - say, a revival service or prophetic conference - it's widely recognized as miraculous manifestation. Could it be that for centuries, organized religion has viewed the concept of energy in all the wrong ways by choosing to define it and label it? Could it be that, in truth, when Jesus spoke of the Kingdom of Heaven being an internal reality, he was speaking of a realm of power and force existent within all things?

I felt led to include this chapter within the book because, in truth, regardless of the labels, the terms, and the definitions we use - regardless of the creeds and dogma one holds - it's impossible to activate faith without energy being present. It's impossible to separate all of those manifestations of the supernatural from the concept of energetic force.

What's referred to as "chi" in many eastern mystic traditions, referring to life force"," is actually closely associated with the Hebrew term "chaim," referring to vitality, health, and wellness - the topic of the toast "la'chaim," meaning "To Health." If you study not only the history of the text of the scriptures but also the traditions of Judaism, you find that even the ancients regarded energy as the very force of life - not only the life that fills the human body but also the life that permeates all things. Could it be that the energy so present within those instantaneous moments of Creation in the very beginning not only became encapsulated into Creation itself but also into the very fabric of humanity? Ancient traditions and philosophies of various cultures seem to be in agreement that this is exactly the case.

By now, I'm sure you realize that the concept of energy is not solely relegated to the faith of Christianity and that God is much larger than the definitions and labels of any religion. However, it's important to note that when awakening comes and when the eyes of understanding become enlightened, as Paul admonished, even understanding of energy within the human body is increased. In the coming months. I'm so pleased to announce that we will be launching the Identity Network Academy School of Prophetic Arts - an entire one-year course for those seekers, like you, who have a passion and burning hunger for the things of God. Within this course, I will be offering an entire month of teachings devoted solely to the concept of energy within the human body. For now, though, it simply is no exaggeration to say that you and I are carriers of the energy of Creation. The same force - the same "power" - which formed the worlds in the very beginning is the exact same power radiating and coursing through your being even now as you read these words.

It's time to awaken to a newer and better understanding of the concept of energy. Energy isn't solely some metaphysical, ethereal force; it's highly personal. When you hold the hand of a loved one, you feel it. Even when you enter into a room filled with strangers, you feel the effects of the energy within others. When was the last time you came in contact with a random stranger on the street and felt that uncomfortable, uneasy feeling? You thought to yourself, he or she had bad "vibes." Well, the fact of the matter is that all throughout the day and night, you and I are always, always sending out very real waves of energy, as you will see. What we call "vibes" are actually confirmation that within us at all times there is the very real, very literal energy of Creation. As we journey together into even greater depths of energy, I want to remind you to become more conscious of your own physical being. Yes; God heals. Yes; the miraculous power of God never stopped flowing. However, just as He is, so are you in thus present world.

And did Jesus himself not say that we are all "gods?" When the Creator first formed and fashioned man from the dust of the ground and breathed into man the very Breathe of Life, causing man to become a living, breathing soul, there was a very real, very literal exchange of energy - a transfer of essence. In fact, in the very moment of infusion, there was literal impartation. The concept of impartation, you see, isn't merely a concept that began in the early days of the Apostolic movement following the Day of Pentecost. No; instead, impartation has always, always been a very real, very natural - very practical - part of every day life experience. Each and every day, you and I are always imparting something - and receiving impartation from those around us. Whether its the energy of the stranger on the street or the smile from the barista at the corner coffee shop or, even more so, the loving touch of a friend or family member, life is filled with moments of energy transference. This truth is as equally practical and as natural as it is metaphysical. As I shared within my book *How Does God Speak?* God is not only speaking to His majestic Creation; God is speaking through His Creation. Often times, in order to see and to feel and to experience the realm of God, you need only to look to your very own life. When you realize that the energy of Heaven is not only around you but is also within you, never again will you be able to view Heaven as some far-away, distant place.

Where is God? In truth, God is within you, God is in your relationships, and God is also surrounding you. As the psalmist said, there is truly no where in existence where the Presence of God is not clearly known and able to be recognized. In writing this, the psalmist was, in fact, saying, the Presence of God is all around. The Kingdom within, quite simply put, is the energy of power and the energy to create. As with all things, though, understanding is needed. The truth of the matter is that with great power, there has always come a need for great responsibility. There has always been energy within you - the powerful force of Creation itself. It's time, now, to start using the energy to your advantage. It's time to not only activate the power but to activate it effectively.

CHAPTER SIX
INFINITE

When I first received the revelation all those years ago of my book *The Universe is at Your Command*, I realized early on how shocking the revelation might seem to the religious, natural mind. It's one thing to say that God is in control; however, it's another matter entirely to say that God has given us the power to create the abundant life for ourselves. It's true, though. Whether you've ever taken the time to realize it yet or not, all things pertaining to life and to godliness - it's all been freely given to you. The Kingdom is within you and, as Jesus said, the same Spirit who is with you is now *within* you. I felt inspired by the Holy Spirit to include this chapter as a way to remind you just how very personal the energy of God truly is. It's as personal as the breathe you breathe and just as natural as the thoughts you think.

What if I were to tell you that there's really no reason for you not to experience the life of your dreams and all that the abundant life entails? What if I were to tell you that you can have the life you truly desire and deserve - that you can have complete health and wellness, increased vitality, better, more satisfying relationships, and even the dream career that you keep envisioning? Would it sound like a fairy tale? It isn't. When you make the willful, conscious decision to become more aware of the energy you possess and begin to become much more responsible and much more active in using that energy to your advantage, just as Jesus said, absolutely nothing will be impossible for you. Truly, the Universe is at your command and all of Heaven and earth are waiting to bring to you all that you desire.

This sentiment isn't merely the fluff of some so-called "New Age" philosophy. It's, in fact, a very real principle within Creation. The very moment - the very instant - God breathed into man the Breathe of Life, causing man to become a living, breathing soul, man, in that instant, became an extension of the Creator Himself - fully endued with the power to manifest and to create. In fact, all of Creation, according to the account in Genesis, is infused with the very essence of God. When the Creator formed and fashioned the earth with His very own words, there was thoughtful, willful intention in the process. This powerful intention not only manifested the worlds within the cosmos, but this intention, by the same token, also created divine precedent, establishing the Law of Creation. "As a man thinketh in his heart, so is he."

In sharing this revelation with you, I would be remiss if I did not include this chapter as a way to say to you that not only is God present for Creation, the Creator is present through Creation. All of Creation, even now, is infused with the Breathe of Life of God, and, as such, the world around you contains the most powerful energy in existence - the power of Creation itself. Creation is not somehow fallen or separated from the energy of the Creator. Creation is, by it's own existence, a manifestation of the power of God. As I've so often said throughout the years, God truly is in all things.

Long before the rise of Christianity and the many other various world religions, it was believed by Jewish mystics that God not only created Creation but that God, in some very literal ways, actually became creation. Such a concept, though shocking to the religious, natural mind, with its limitations and preconceived notions of God, is actually not as outlandish as it may seem at first glance. When the psalmist spoke of the Presence of God being all-present, all-encompassing, and ever-expansive, he was speaking of a very literal, very real energy of infinity. Even as you read these words, every atom, every molecule of your being and also of the world around you is pulsating, moving, and vibrating with the energy of God. There is truly no separation between God and man - or between the Creator and His wonderful Creation.

Could it be that science and even the advancements continuously being made in research serve to only confirm what the ancients knew all along - that everything is energy because literally everything is God? Such a statement is offensive to the natural mind, steeped in the illusion of separation and dualism. When was the last time you heard a sincere believer say something along the lines of, "God's not in that?" Or, ""That can't be God." It never ceases to amaze me just how futile organized religion truly is. With it's illusion of separation, it's nothing more than a guessing game - a game of "let's try to find God." My friend and fellow seeker, never even once have you ever been separated from God. And never has your life ever been without the *energeo* of God's loving, creative power. In fact, it's all around you even now within this beautiful creation! If you truly desire to see God, to hear God, and to experience God, you only need to open your eyes and look around!

When I began to receive the revelation that would ultimately become the books *The Universe is at Your Command* and *Creating with Your Thoughts*, I knew well just how controversial the revelations would seem to the religious, natural mind. The religious mind, you see, because of the illusion of separation and the illusion of the "sin" nature, always looks for power elsewhere. Rather than looking within to find the Kingdom, the religious mind causes individuals to always look externally - to buildings, to rituals, to prayers - always in search of the ever-elusive "move of God." As a result, many a sincere and well-intentioned believer have traveled to the ends of the earth, from place to place and from city to city - from church to church, even - in search of "revival." It's exhausting, isn't it? The need to always look for the glory outside of yourself? When Jesus spoke of the Kingdom being within, I can imagine that there were many religious mindsets offended even in his day.

One of the many catalysts which propelled me to write *The Universe is at Your Command*, aside from the powerful, heavenly Law of Attraction, was the shocking, startling reality that early Jewish mystics never considered the term "God" to be a noun or even a subject. Rather, they wholeheartedly believed "God" to be a verb - a term of action and movement. We find this even in the account of Creation, as recorded in the Book of Genesis. In the very beginning, even when there was nothing, the Spirit of God "moved" upon the face of the deep. Even when there was nothing, there was movement. There was the energy of God. And long before man was ever formed and fashioned from the dust of the ground, even then, there was the inescapable, infinite force that would soon be breathed into his lungs. Today, that same power of movement is alive and well, living within you. It's always been.

How can the eternal, infinite power of God be defined or reduced to human words? How can one even begin to articulate the expansiveness of the energy so present within the force that created the earth and all existence in the very beginning? The ancient Jewish mystics of old regarded the concept of God as *Ein Sof,* meaning "The Endlessness." Truly, God is in all things because all things have come from God. And it is from that infinite, energetic source of loving power than literally everything in existence exists. This includes even the daily moments of your life.

The Gospel according to John seems to denote this in a very mystical sort of way, referencing even the voice and the energetic move of God very transcendentally, noting that before anything else was ever even formed, there was the Word. Without this Word, there was nothing made that was made, according to the writer of John. Paul, even in Colossians references this fact, writing, *For by him were all things created, that are in heaven, and that are in earth, visible and invisible. (Colossians 1:16 KJV)* Though the terminology used was different, it seems that even the early church regarded the power of God in quite a forceful way - a force of movement and activity.

In the beginning was the Word, and the Word was with God, and the Word was God.

2 The same was in the beginning with God.

3 All things were made by him; and without him was not any thing made that was made.

4 In him was life; and the life was the light of men.

5 And the light shineth in darkness; and the darkness comprehended it not.

6 There was a man sent from God, whose name was John.

7 The same came for a witness, to bear witness of the Light, that all men through him might believe.

8 He was not that Light, but was sent to bear witness of that Light.

9 That was the true Light, which lighteth every man that cometh into the world.

10 He was in the world, and the world was made by him, and the world knew him not.

11 He came unto his own, and his own received him not.

12 But as many as received him, to them gave he power to become the sons of God, even to them that believe on his name:

13 Which were born, not of blood, nor of the will of the flesh, nor of the will of man, but of God.

14 And the Word was made flesh, and dwelt among us, (and we beheld his glory, the glory as of the only begotten of the Father,) full of grace and truth. (John 1:1-14 KJV)

Within the words of the Gospel of John, we find a reference to the literal energy of creative force not only creating but also becoming - the Word *became* flesh and dwelt among us. Could this seemingly cryptic text allude to not only the incarnation of Jesus but, even more so, speak of the incarnation of the Spirit into all things in existence? Could it be that when referencing incarnation, the early writers knew instinctively that God literally *became* Creation, infusing His Creation with the very essence of Himself? Suffice it to say, the force of creative energy so present in the initial moments of creation is still moving, still vibrant, and still ever-expanding. But what does this reveal to us about the nature of God?

What the writer of the Gospel of John referenced as "The Word" is, in fact, the very literal energy of God's creative power. *Without him there was nothing made that was made.* This passage, in many ways, serves not only to illustrate the infinite nature of God but also, to some extent, even depict the infinite energy of God's power within Creation itself. When the worlds were formed and when man was created from the dust of the ground, the Creator, in those moments of creating, didn't solely craft objects that he desired to see; He infused all things with the very essence of His own self. And by doing so, there were very real principles and universal, heavenly Laws established. Even in the very beginning of it all, we find the power of intention illustrated - that where there is thought, there is energy and great force to create.

To put it another way, where there is thought - where there is consciousness - there is energy and movement. There is vitality. There is the act of Creation itself. In Genesis 1, we are introduced to the Holy Spirit, the *Ruach Kodes*h, and we find movement, as the Spirit of God *moved* upon the face of the deep. The writer of the Book of Hebrews defines the Word of God as something not only "living" but as something also "quick" and "active." And, yet, in some way, even the very nature of God Himself is so intrinsically interwoven into the force of creative energy that it is almost impossible to separate God from the act of Creation. Where there is God, there is always the potential to create and to re-create. Where God is, there is limitless potential and possibility. Truly, He makes all things new, as the scriptures remind us.

To further illustrate this, though, it's interesting the writings of even the Prophet Isaiah - a prophet who prophesied centuries before the birth of Jesus. In the recorded words of Isaiah, we find an illustration of the powerful force of God's creative energy depicted even more precisely - interestingly enough by a reminder to look for God in natural space and time, here in the physical world around us. *Look up to the sky! Who created all these heavenly lights? He is the one who leads out their ranks; he calls them all by name. Because of his absolute power and awesome strength, not one of them is missing. (Isaiah 40:26)* This verse speaks of God's creative power but also of God's power to maintain existence itself. You see, not only is the force of God responsible for creating all that we see, but it's also solely responsible for maintaining all that we see. This cosmic, universal force of God is responsible for sustaining all life and for keeping everything in perfect balance and alignment. As you will see, though, this also has equally as much to do with us as it does with the Creator. The above referenced verse uses the phrase "absolute power;" however, in the New Living Translation, the phrase used is actually "dynamic energy" instead. How very fitting. But what does this force of God truly have to do with daily life upon Planet Earth? Can this force be harnessed and used within our own lives? If so, how does one access it? Howe does one harness it?

As you will see, the power of God working in you is also the power of God working all around you. It's the same power. By realizing that you've never at one time ever truly been separated from the infinite nature of God, not only will you experience a greater measure of the energy of God but will, in turn, also recognize your own power to create the abundant life. As I detail within my book *Manifesting: The World You Desire*, with great power has always come a great responsibility. You have been given a role to play. Even as you read these words, the power within you is active quick, and dynamic. Your mission within the Kingdom, should you choose to accept it, is to learn to make that power more effective within your life. Then and only then will all things become possible to you, just as the Christ promises.

CHAPTER SEVEN
THE SPIRIT IN SCIENCE

Everything within Creation is moving. It's active. It's vibrant. It's ever-expanding. And, as such, it's always evolving and always, continuously being re-shaped and reformed. The world today is not the world of yesterday. Truly, as the scriptures remind us, all things are made new - day by day and moment by moment. It's impossible to speak of the energy of God without also speaking of the elements of growth and change - of evolution.

Something truly remarkable, truly magical begins to happen when the mind becomes renewed and when the old religious mind is stripped away, leaving only the lens of limitlessness. We begin to not only see God in new and in revelatory ways but we also become more able to see the effects of the energy of God all around us. Those things that once so seemed coincidental and so random, when viewed through the lens of religion, suddenly, in an instant, begin to seem much more divinely aligned and so divinely orchestrated. Those things that once seemed to make very little sense at all, suddenly, when awakening comes, begin to seem so divinely inspired. And, as awakening comes, we see God in operation all around us.

From the very beginning, mankind has longed to better understand the meaning and the nature of life itself. For this reason, many worldviews have been crafted and re-crafted - shaped and re-shaped. With greater knowledge and with greater experience comes, also, a greater ability to learn. Truly, the knowledge of the glory of the LORD is covering the earth as the waters cover the sea. As man has grown in his understanding of the things of God, great advancements have been made in research. Where science is concerned, studies of the natural world have evolved throughout the ages, as man has come to greater understanding and greater enlightenment. Today, we know more than we knew twenty years ago - or even ten years ago. But man has always possessed an inner hunger to know and to better understand the mechanics of the natural world. This ever-increasing knowledge has caused many a great paradigm shift within global consciousness throughout the ages, with each breakthrough leading only to more breakthrough and to even newer, more revelatory discoveries. As the old adage goes, "as above, so below." Meaning, simply, that there has always been a great connectedness where science and God are concerned. The heavens declare the glory of God, and the glory of God is revealed all the more, the more we study this gift of life - and the energy surrounding it.

As I've so often said throughout the years, all knowledge must be tested. Knowledge is ever-increasing and ever-expanding. With new experiences come greater levels of insight and better, clearer ways by which to view the world. Suffice it to say, we're always learning something new. Nowhere is this truth any more true than where science is concerned. For centuries, mankind has longed to better, more comprehensively understand the power at work in what Isaiah referred to as "dynamic energy." There's something holding all of existence together. What is it?

Even in the time of the ancients, particularly in Greece, there were many thinkers and many great philosophers who sought to better understand the mechanics at work within the natural world. With every philosophy, though, something altogether different continued to be revealed - that it's impossible to deal with energy without also beginning to deal with the concept of spirituality. I felt inspired by the Holy Spirit to include this chapter within the book because, as you will soon realize, all throughout the ages, with every advancement in science and with every new discovery, the Spirit has always been present, leading us toward greater understanding. It's truly no exaggeration to say that when we hunger for understanding, the very hunger itself is the inner force of God at work. Truly, if we seek, we will find. And if we knock, doorways will become opened to us.

Throughout the ages, what's become clear is that there is some connection between the physical and the spiritual world - that existence itself is somewhat spiritual and the force holding it all together is directly related to existence. Metaphysics is the philosophical study of the mechanics at work within the Universe. It deals with the "first order" of things. Metaphysics, though, is equally as spiritual as it is scientific and philosophical, and it's equally as transcendent as it is natural. When you begin to question the energies at work within Creation, what you begin to find more and more is that the very very questions themselves lead one to deeper levels of spirituality - every question leading toward even greater discoveries. Somewhere in the midst of the searching, though, it begins to become clear that the nature of God is so clearly interconnected to the nature of man that to better understand the nature of God man must look within himself. Metaphysics, in a nutshell, is the reminder to us that when Jesus spoke of the Kingdom of God being an internal reality, he was speaking quite literally and not merely metaphorically.

There truly is a power - an energy - at work within you and all around you. In the 4th century BCE, it was the philosopher Aristotle who wrote a dissertation on "cause and effect" referring to what he termed "first philosophy," "first wisdom," and "first theology." When the writings were later transcribed in the 1st century BCE, the writings were titled *Ta meta ta physika*, meaning, "the ones about nature." This served to help lay the foundation of what we now refer to as the study of "physics." This isn't speaking of the brand of science that we now call "physics" within the more modern world, though. Aristotle's dissertations dealt primarily with the philosophy of the natural world, more so than the actual science. The Latin noun "metaphysica" was used to title

Aristotle's works, leading to the branch of philosophy that we now would refer to as metaphysics.

In Aristotle's writings, he dealt primarily with the philosophy of "being," researching the ideas of "the first causes of things." Today, the term metaphysics is used in a much broader way than in those days of Aristotle. Through every philosophical persuasion, though, there has always been a hint of the spiritual where the study of existence is concerned. It's almost as if the Spirit has been so desirous of being found that He's included hints all along the way - each one leading to a greater, even deeper level of spiritual awakening. Something powerful happens when you ask questions. Always question, my friend, and never ever stop.

Many beliefs regarding the physics of existence were challenged at the end of the seventeenth century, however. It was at this time that Newtonian physics became the chief cornerstone of man's understanding of physics and the teachings of Sir Isaac Newton became central in man's search of understanding. It was through Newtonian physics that man began to understand more clearly a very specific set of universal laws at work within the Universe - laws that are concrete and immovable. For instance, the law of gravity was one such law within Newton's discoveries. The discoveries of Sir Isaac Newton helped to lay even more of the framework by which humanity understands the mechanics at work within the natural, physical world of space and time.

Knowledge, indeed, like the waters cover the sea, continued to expand, though. Even newer discoveries were made as mankind continued to question and to search. With each discovery came an even greater measure of clarity. Perceptions, also, began to become shifted. This continues even today. As I've said for years, there will always be "more" of God. Regardless how much experience, how much insight, and how much revelation one receives, there will always, always be more. There's always more to see and to discover in this marvelous, beautiful existence called life. With each new experience and with each discovery comes also greater revelation and understanding of man's connection with the energies of the Universe. Physics, in some way, seems to confirm that we are not only living within a physical, natural world but that we ourselves possess the same energy within us that makes up the physicality of the world around us.

It was the discoveries and advancements made by Sir Isaac Newton that gave humanity a glimpse, even more deeply, into the mechanics of the tapestry of physical existence. According to his theories, the Universe operates like clockwork - according to very specific, highly detailed, calculated laws. The advancements in research didn't stop there, though. Then came the The New Science. In the early part of the twentieth century, even more questions were asked and new discovered made - these discoveries even more shocking. It was around this time that advancements were being made in the arena of quantum physics - a field of study that says that all matter is made entirely of energy. Quantum mechanics rose from the findings of Max Planck in 1900 in his solution to radiation. It was also around this time that Albert Einstein, in 1905, offered a paper detailing even more the energy of quantum mechanics, researching the photoelectric effect - noting the correlation between energy and light. In this time, there also came the theories of the mid-1920's with Erwin Shcrodinger, Werner Heisenberg, and Max Born and many others. As mankind continued to question the role of energy within the physical, natural world, other startling discoveries were made which seemed to prove beyond a reasonable doubt that not only is everything composed of energy but that we have the power to influence this energy in some way - that the energy isn't independent of us but is, rather, interconnected with us.

But then came the most startling discovery of all with the rise of quantum physics. Quantum physics proves, undeniably, that, shockingly, physical matter doesn't even truly exist at all! Yes; you read that correctly. It's through quantum physics that we find the startling truth that even the physicality of the natural world is merely energy moving at different velocities - that atoms are vibrating at different rates of speed, creating merely the illusion of physicality. This is the most startling, most shocking advancement of all, as we enter into this more modern era with the understanding that not only is the natural world nothing more than energy but that we, ourselves, are made of that exact same energy. Could this have been what the Apostle Paul referenced when he wrote of the invisible realms, speaking of Christ being above all, in all, and even through all? It would seem so. It would appear, even, that the early church, even through different terminology, recognized the great universal, heavenly connection at work within Creation. I share much more of this theory in my book *Synchronicities: God's Universal Tools*. Suffice it to say, when Paul spoke of all things "working together," he was speaking of more than just the matters of daily, physical life. He was speaking of some greater, more innate, more intrinsic power flowing through us.

You see, my friend and fellow seeker, even from the very beginning, the truth has existed in plain sight right before our very eyes. And when spiritual awakening comes and when the natural, religious mind is renewed and crafted to the things of the Spirit, suddenly, the veil becomes stripped away. We find that not only is the energy of God working within us and through us but that it always has been., When awakening comes and when the eyes of our understanding become "enlightened," as Paul wrote, we begin to find that there truly is a power working in us - the energy of creative force. This power working within us is truly greater than the world - because, in actuality, its the exact same force which created the world in the very beginning of it all.

For I long to see you, that I may impart unto you some spiritual gift, to the end ye may be established;

12 That is, that I may be comforted together with you by the mutual faith both of you and me.

13 Now I would not have you ignorant, brethren, that oftentimes I purposed to come unto you, (but was let hitherto,) that I might have some fruit among you also, even as among other Gentiles.

14 I am debtor both to the Greeks, and to the Barbarians; both to the wise, and to the unwise.

15 So, as much as in me is, I am ready to preach the gospel to you that are at Rome also.

16 For I am not ashamed of the gospel of Christ: for it is the power of God unto salvation to every one that believeth; to the Jew first, and also to the Greek.

17 For therein is the righteousness of God revealed from faith to faith: as it is written, The just shall live by faith.

18 For the wrath of God is revealed from heaven against all ungodliness and unrighteousness of men, who hold the truth in unrighteousness;

19 Because that which may be known of God is manifest in them; for God hath shewed it unto them.

20 For the invisible things of him from the creation of the world are clearly seen, being understood by the things that are made, even his eternal power and

Godhead; so that they are without excuse:

21 Because that, when they knew God, they glorified him not as God, neither were thankful; but became vain in their imaginations, and their foolish heart was darkened.

22 Professing themselves to be wise, they became fools,

23 And changed the glory of the uncorruptible God into an image made like to corruptible man, and to birds, and fourfooted beasts, and creeping things. (Romans 1:11-23 KJV)

In Paul's epistle to the church at Rome, we find an illustration of this great power at work when he references the "invisible things." In verses 19 and

20, we find what is perhaps the most blatant assertion that the power of the invisible world is not only within us but that we have the power to harness it. *For the invisible things of him from the creation of the world are clearly seen, being understood by the things that are made, even his eternal power and Godhead; so that they are without excuse: Because that, when they knew God, they glorified him not as God, neither were thankful; but became vain in their imaginations, and their foolish heart was darkened.* Within the text, Paul seems to state that the invisible things of the invisible world can actually be seen and experienced - that the power can become effective in some way within our lives. He writes that the imagination is the only thing keeping us from being able to actually see and to experience the realm of the invisible within our lives.

And so here, within even the writings of the Apostle Paul, we find reference to the power of the mind and are given a glimpse of the responsibility we've been entrusted with to actually harness the energy of Creation around us. It is through our thoughts and through our imaginations that the power within becomes activated and manifests within the physical, natural world. For as long as you've had breath within your lungs - and even before, in all honesty - you've possessed within your very own being the power of energy which created the world and all that's in it. Yet, for far too long you've failed to realize just how truly powerful, how very infinite and limitless you are. When awakening comes, though, nothing shall be impossible to you. Not only is power present, but power can be used.

CHAPTER EIGHT
FREQUENCY AND VIBRATION

To say that thoughts become things isn't just some cliche or spiritual mantra of encouragement designed to help us "think happy thoughts." There's a misnomer of sorts at work within the field of spirituality that seems to suggest rather erroneously that we're always supposed to be floating on clouds - always happy, always feeling good, and never ever having a bad day. And while we're at it, why not throw in images of cute, fluffy bunnies and rainbows, and unicorns. Well, if you're reading these words, I'm going to assume that you're a conscious being, and I'm going to assume that if you've lived in a physical world for any amount of time at all then you know life just doesn't work that way. There are moments that feel good, and there are those many moments that feel not so good. It's all part of life in the Kingdom.

What if I were to tell you, though, that through it all, you're actually the one creating the story of it all? What if I were to say that even those moments you consider so "bad," even in those moments you have a role to play - and that you've always played it, even then? At first, such a claim may seem quite offensive. It may even cause anger, to some degree. "Jeremy, are you saying that I caused even the bad in my life?" Well, what I'm saying, my friend, is that what would life be like if you actually chose to become more responsible with your thoughts? This isn't some "fluff" or pseudo-science when we speak of thoughts becoming things; it's a very real universal, very heavenly Law - that even in the moments that feel "bad," we're still creating even then. I've said for years that thoughts become things, and I know it to be true. I feel inspired by the Holy Ghost to include for you this chapter because it's time you realize, once and for all, exactly why that it.

We know that thoughts have power. We know that our beliefs manifest and bring to us accordingly. We even know that when we change our minds, we literally change our lives. But why is that, exactly? What is it that causes this to be the case? Knowing the reason not only causes us to become even more aware, but it causes us to become even more powerful - and equally as responsible with the power we've awakened to.

Years ago, when I realized the immense power residing within my thoughts, it changed my life. As I've said for years, though, to know something is one thing; however, to truly understand something is another matter entirely. It's not enough to simply believe that your thoughts create things and manifest for you. You need to know why it happens and what's causing it. Because when you do, you'll not only be able to make that power more "effective" in your daily life, but you'll also begin to create the life you've always dreamed of.

And, after all, isn't that the promise of an abundant life? You've lived far, far beneath your means for far, far too long, and there's a reason for it. The reason is simply a lack of alignment and nothing more. Allow me to explain.

You've always had the power to have and to get exactly what you want. Like God, you're a powerful Creator, and you always have been. Even Jesus himself said that we are all "gods." And, as the scriptures remind us, just as He is, so are we in this present world. So, it's not a far stretch of the imagination to say that we've been entrusted with unlimited, abounding power to create - and to attract. There's a reason, though, why the Law of Attraction is so heavenly and so powerful, and to better understand the mechanics at work behind it requires a better understanding of other universal already in existence within the thought - and possess the same energy as the thought itself. You've seen this truth confirmed over and over again countless times throughout your life, even if you weren't always aware of it. When the argument with the coworker happened at the beginning of the day or when the driver cut you off in traffic, the feeling of anger and frustration stayed with you for hours - perhaps even for the rest of the day. And that time you had the argument with your significant other, the feeling of worry, dread, and gloom followed you long after the conversation ended and the words spoken. Why is this the case? Because the "vibes" of intention which fueled those exchanges are even more real than the moments they were a part of. Like ripples within a pond when a stone is thrown, these ripples of energy remain long, long after the initial moments of impact. And with all thoughts, we've been given a very real choice. I share much more about the mechanics behind thoughts in *Creating with Your Thoughts*, detailing how all throughout life, you and I are, by divine design, given front row seats to the thoughts we think. The reason for this, quite simply, is because when thoughts are focused upon, they expand and continue to grow. That's why feelings remain as long as they do. Your feelings, in fact, are a very real indicator of what you're creating at any given moment. And so, when you change your thoughts, you're literally changing your life in that you're changing the "vibes" harnessed within those thoughts. Picture this for a moment. Do moments of time manifest when they happen, or do they manifest, first, the very moment they're thought of and focused upon? As an example, Jesus said that when we lust in our hearts it's as if we've already committed sin - revealing to us that, where thoughts are concerned, there's really a point of connection between the manifestation and the very thought behind it.

The business you've been dreaming of creating - it's actually already created. You simply haven't put action into making it a reality in the three-dimensional world. The same can be said of, well, literally everything in life. The new home already exists, the new, more fulfilling, more satisfying relationship, and everything else all exists within the realm of thought and within the realm of belief. That being said, why then does it often times seem so impossible to bring the desire into the physical, natural world? Allow me to ask it another way. Why does it often seem so difficult to hold in your hands the dreams and the desires within your heart?

The Law of Attraction is very real, and it's changed not only my life but also the lives of literally millions throughout the world for the better when it's recognized and utilized. Interestingly enough, though, as popular as "the secret" of the Law of Attraction is, the Law of Attraction is actually a secondary Law; the primary Law by which it operates is the Law of Vibration. We literally are moving at all times - moving in an ocean of continuous motion. All throughout existence, at any given time, there's movement. Atoms are continuously buzzing about, creating frequency through movement. When was the last time you referred to your rather free-spirited friend as being "high-vibe?" Well, believe it or not, there's something to that. Every thought emanates very real energy - energy that matches specific frequencies.

Sarah Prout, author of *Dear Universe: 200 Mini Meditations for Instant Manifestations* writes in an article entitled "How to Manifest Anything You Want with the Law of Vibration," *Most people don't know how to manifest properly because they don't fully understand how The Law of Vibration works. The Law of Vibration is one of the most important Universal laws to contemplate. Quite often people focus upon The Law of Attraction, but the real power source behind manifesting your desires is in fact, The Law of Vibration.*

That's where all of the fun, magical elements come into play. Your goal? You want to raise your vibration, train your vibration and program your vibration to create a magnificent life you love. The possibilities are endless.

The Law of Vibration states that anything that exists in our universe, whether visible or not, can be quantified as a frequency or an energetic pattern. From teeny tiny atoms, to rainbows, light, stardust, dust on butterfly wings and happy thoughts – to more dense matter like rock, thousand year old trees, dirt, bones, diamonds and metal – they all carry their own unique vibration. We live in an ocean of motion. Everything is buzzing around and clumping together with things that match up in the frequency department. It's like a big game of 'Go Fish'.

Everything in the entire Universe carries a certain frequency. It oscillates at its own unique set point, drawing that which is like itself into a central orbit. As the old saying goes: "Birds of a feather, flock together." To simplify this, think of it this way...as you choose happy feelings, more happy feelings will be drawn into vibrational harmony with the frequency you are offering. If you are constantly cranky and upset, then you will be creating more of the same into your experience. It works like a big mirror. You create your vibrational set point, buzz that frequency out into the ether and whatever your dominant energetic patterns are will be drawn to you in the form of things, people and experiences that are in alignment with your vibration set point.

Sprout continues, *By consciously sculpting your energy (your vibration) you ACTIVATE and work with The Law of Vibration to deliberately manifest. You do this by seeking out ways to optimize your energy and clear the way for the alignment process to work its magic. By aligning with your desires and trusting that that have already manifested on the etheric plane, means that you release the resistance and the Universe can deliver your goodies because you have created the space. In order to manifest more abundance into your life you need to be ready to SPARK a deeper connection with the Universe.* You see, positive thoughts aren't just the fluff of some pseudo-science masquerading as spirituality. The reality is that there's nothing more powerful - or more heavenly - than the thoughts you think. As a divine, co-creator with God, you've been infused with the very power of the Godhead. Just like Jesus, you're the image of the invisible God and within you dwells all the power of the Godhead bodily. Just as Jesus said when teaching concerning the Kingdom of God, whatsoever things you desire, when you believe it, you will receive it. The issue for far too long, though, has been that you've either not been completely aware of your beliefs or have held to beliefs that, whether you know it or not, haven't always been in your best interest. Hear me when I say that absolutely nothing in existence will hinder you from manifesting quite like religion. It's deadly. It's an illusion. When you view yourself as being separate from the rest of the world - and separate from that dream job and that dream home - not only are you setting up mental barriers within your mind, but you're actually, in turn, attracting the very opposite of what you claim to want. The Universe has always given to you exactly what you've decreed and commanded, according to your thoughts and beliefs and, like a self-fulfilling prophecy of sorts, when you've felt disconnected from God and have felt unworthy and undeserving, you've created only more lack and more insecurity within your very own life. It's divine Law. As a man thinketh in his heart, so is he.

In closing, let me offer to you this word of encouragement - and a word of advice. You've always possessed within you the exact same power that created the Universe and all that's in it. With this power, though, comes also a tremendous responsibility to become more aware of the role you're playing within your very own life. Chances are, even as you read these words, the life that you now lead doesn't feel very satisfying. In fact, chances are your life feels anything but "good." As you dream of the future, there's so much more that you want. We've all been there. When you become more aware of the role you're playing within your own life, though, not only will you begin to see the world around you in a much different way than ever before but all the sudden, all of those things that once seemed to be so impossible and so utterly far-away begin to become even more of a reality. As Paul said, there truly is a power at work in you. My advice to you would be, simply, learn to use it to your own advantage.

CHAPTER NINE
THE MIRACULOUS MIND

My sincere prayer for you, my friend and fellow seeker, is that by now you've begun to view the energy of the Universe in a much, much different, much more expansive and much more all-encompassing way than ever before. I pray also that now that you've developed a better sense of awareness where energy is concerned that you would, in turn, begin to be a little less religiously-minded than before. I say that not to cast judgment upon your beliefs, but to say, simply, you've always been much, much more unlimited than you've ever truly given yourself credit for. When awakening comes and when the old paradigms of limitation and self-doubt become stripped away and replaced with the Divine Mind of the Spirit, all of the sudden, the entirety of the world begins to look much more like an awfully grand adventure and less like some burden or chore. The abundant life truly isn't as far away as it might seem at the current moment.

Even as I write these words to you, I find myself reminded of the many, many examples I've witnessed firsthand throughout the years - stories of lives that were radically changed and bodies physically healed the moment seekers just like you began to harness the power of energy. Lives were transformed - sometimes even instantaneously. And through it all, little by little, the old paradigms of limitation and self-doubt were stripped away and replaced by the great force of the infinite. Today, even as you read these words, you're being presented with a choice - a choice to either remain in complacency, settling for a religious worldview steeped in the illusion of separation or move, instead, into the abundance of all that awaits you. The choice, as with all things, is completely your very own. Personally, I choose life.

What I learned all those years ago within my own life and ministry is that life truly can be as "dynamic" as you intend for it to be. It can be just as miraculous as the many stories within the Book of Acts, and it can be even more real. When you stop thinking of the realm of God as some far-off, distant ream and begin to realize that the same God who formed the Universe and all that's within it is the same God who lives through you - *as* you - never again will testimonies be reserved solely for other people from ages long-since passed. One of my many, many joys is seeing lives transformed when seekers, just like you, begin to reclaim their own dynamic energy - when they realize, once and for all, that Heaven is whatever they make it because Heaven has always, always been within them. Life is not only transformed when we begin to harness the energy of God within us, but life, in turn, naturally begins to become much more abundant.

But it's not enough to simply have the power to change. It's not enough to simply even know that you possess the power to transform. The power must be implemented. You have to actually do something. As the writer of the Book of James reminds us, it's not enough even to simply believe. We must do. And so, where the energy of the Kingdom of God is concerned, what exactly are we to do with it? And how does the power become activated?

Allow me to ask it another way. Right now, living and breathing, residing within you is the power of Creation itself. But how do you take that power and truly begin to make it more "effective" within your life? The energy within you and the energy around you is activated, harnessed, and controlled entirely through your thoughts and beliefs. With literally each and every passing thought, all throughout the day, you're becoming a literal superconductor of the energies within Creation. Knowing this is only half the journey, though. Activation of the energy isn't enough. Implementation is key.

To say that thoughts become things is true, as it's with our thoughts that we're literally harnessing the power of creative energy within us and around us. However, all too often, where most fail to actually become more effective in their creative processes is they become forgetful of the power they truly possess. It's all too common, really, and I've seen it firsthand throughout more than twenty years of prophetic ministry. It's not enough to think the thought; you must maintain the thought. You must hold fast to the thought you're wanting to enact. And, while holding on to it and maintaining it, you're going to have to begin to put action to it. It's then and only then that the energies of the Universe will be working in tandem with you and not against you. There's a reason the scriptures admonish believers to "hold fast" to the profession of faith. It's speaking of more than just words; it's speaking of literally every passing thought.

There's such a unique, such an intrinsic correlation between thought and energy that it's literally impossible to ever truly separate the two. You and I are literally hardwired - biologically, even - to harness the energy within the Universe to bring about our desires and our decrees. You have no choice but to create with your thoughts because, like God, you're a divine being. You've never been a physical being seeking to have a spiritual experience. No;

instead, you've always been a powerful, omnipotent, spiritual being, here to have a physical experience. The fact of the matter is that your energy has always been "effective," though, even when it may have been seemingly creating the opposite of your desired, supposedly intended results. Suffice it to say that you're always creating something.

For far too long, though, most have created haphazardly and flippantly without very much conscious thought. There's a reason why the Book of James speaks of the dangers of being double-minded. According to the Book of James, double-minded people are unstable in all their ways. What does this double-mindedness look like in practicality? It looks a lot like complaining about not having the life you desire while waiting for God to one day bless you. It looks a lot like always talking about having more money but for years continuously putting off starting your own business - the one you keep dreaming about. Double-mindedness looks a lot like feeling lonely and complaining about not having a relationship while at the same time spending your days on the sofa, in front of the television, waiting for a relationship to just fall into your lap. To put it simply, double-mindedness looks a lot like hypocrisy.

It's possible to be hypocritical even without being fully, consciously aware of it. Where the energy of God is concerned, though, the energy never lies. It always knows the truth. It always knows the deepest, most innate motive and truest thought. This is why the scriptures speaks of the Spirit being a discerner of the thoughts and the intentions of the heart. The truth of the matter is that it's impossible to truly master your creative power and to cause the energy of God to work in alignment with you without, first, really getting to know yourself - the real, true "you" and not the version religion or society or culture has programmed you to be. When Jesus spoke of the realm of God being a Kingdom within, he wasn't speaking in mystical, allegorical terms. No; he was speaking literally, in fact.

Energy is harnessed through thought and through intention - through inner, deeper motives. What I so often share with clients throughout the world who come to me for prophetic insight is that mastering your true, inner power to create the life of your dreams begins by discovering the "hidden things." What are those hidden thoughts and motives keeping you from discovering your true power? What are those deeper, hidden, more secret fears and insecurities and barriers keeping you from truly awakening to the person you've been called to be? Hear me when I say that you aren't going to be able to truly master the energy around you until you first learn to master the energy within you. Heaven, just as Jesus said, has always been the realm within - the realm of motive, thought, belief, and intention.

In closing this chapter, I want to encourage you to begin to go deeper than ever before - deeper into the realm of the Kingdom. You do this by going deeper into your own self. What you will find is that, when you do, not only will you begin to realize that you've always had a very real role to play within the unfolding of your life's story, but that you've been cast in the role of a lifetime, actually - cast as a leading star. No one else can play the part you've been cast to play except for you. A great story is unfolding all around you each and very day. The question is when will you begin to actively participate in your own life?

CHAPTER TEN
MASTERY

As we've journeyed together throughout the pages of this book, into the ancient secrets of some of history's greatest principles regarding energy, what we've learned is that energy is not only all around us but that it is truly all there is. In answering the question of where is God in it, the answer is a resounding, "Everywhere." He is the energy of Creation itself, as well as the manifestation. He is the inner desire, as well as the thought surrounding it. He is the dream, the realization of the dream, as well as the entire journey toward the manifestation of that dream. He is truly LORD of all. Throughout the ages, though man has long-since desired to gain better understanding of the energy of God, the reality is that man has often-times been his very own worst enemy in the process. When you live life from the place of the illusion of separation rather than from the togetherness and the great, majestic connectedness within existence, not only does the abundant life seem so very far away but, from the perspective of the illusion of separation and from the dualistic dichotomy that it creates, judgments are formed within the natural mind. As a result, rather than striving to become more aware of our own energy, we strive to judge the energies of others - as if it's out place to do so. "God isn't in that," we say. "There wasn't a part of God in that." "He was out of God's will when they divorced." "She couldn't possibly have been in the will of God." In the never ending game of religion, it always looks so very black and white, doesn't it?

The Kingdom of God, though, is a realm of color and of diversity. You can experience the power of God in a yoga studio as equally, if not more so, than you can in a revival service at a church. You can experience the realm of God while walking down the street or when listening to a song or even when experiencing what seems to be the very worst day of your life. And so can everyone else. How often we forget that.

The energy of God is the universal reminder to humanity that we're all on equal footing, regardless of where we've come from - that we've all been given the same measure of the unlimited nature of an eternal God. In fact, the same creative energy that causes one individual to begin the successful company is the exact same energy that, for another, when not recognized, continues the life of poverty, lack, and struggle. The issue has never been the measure of power residing within your life; the issue has always been your recognition of it and your ability to harness it to your advantage. It's time to bring about the success you deserve. It's time to bring about a more abundant life.

Bestselling author Jack Canfield, author of *Chicken Soup for the Soul*, describes the powerful energy of attraction in this way: *What you think about, talk about, believe strongly about, and feel intensely about, you will bring about.* Canfield has always been open about his use of the Law of Attraction to bring about his publishing success. All throughout the world, millions, just like you, have found the secret to success and have learned to manifest a more abundant, more fulfilling life. But it really is no secret any longer. You are entirely responsible for your life, because you are entirely responsible for your thoughts and beliefs. You are the only one capable of creating the life you desire.

It was Henry Ford who famously said, *Whether you think you can or you think you can't - you're right.* Whether you know it or not, you've always been right, and your beliefs have brought to you exactly what you've intended. For far too long, though, you've not been fully aware of the intention hidden behind those beliefs. In fact, it's never truly been that your beliefs have been wrong. It's just that for far too long those beliefs have never truly served to bring about your greatest, highest, most heavenly good. Whether "good" or "bad," though, you've always been right and you've always had exactly what you've believed in. This "secret," it would seem, is the same secret that throughout the ages has given rise to kingdoms and to corporations, brought divine healing, built lasting wealth, attracted relationships, and brought about lasting change. This secret, in fact, even served to establish the miraculous church - a church clothed in matchless power.

You can't speak of energy without speaking of power, and you can't speak of power without, also, speaking of the realm of thought and belief. Even as you read these words, even now, there's a gift in you - a very real treasure - that is activated with each and every passing thought. All throughout the day and night, this gift stirs within you, constantly crying out to the Universe and to the physical world around you. It makes demands. It makes decrees. It doesn't merely wish or hope for; it simply *knows*. This gift knows that it can have anything it desires. It knows how very unlimited it is. This inner gift of power knows that *all* things are possible.

When Jesus went about doing good and healing all who were oppressed of the devil, he wasn't merely sharing the message of the Kingdom by saying it; he was sharing it by showing it. All throughout the ages, in various cultures throughout time, regardless of belief or creed, the power within has always been showing itself in many varied and unique ways. It's given rise to the empires of kings and has toppled equally as many. It has sparked many great philosophies throughout the ages, igniting intrigue and passionate discovery of the invisible realms - always driving man toward a greater knowledge and understanding of his true, unlimited nature. From even the very beginning of it all, there has always been something innate within man that has always wanted to better understand the forces at work behind the scenes.

Wallace D. Wattles, author of *The Science of Getting Rich*, said, *By thought, the thing you want is brought to you; by action, you receive it.* In a December,

2019 article for *Forbes* entitled "How To Use The Law Of Attraction To Manifest Your Dream Job," Caroline Castrillon writes, *The Law of Attraction isn't magic, and it isn't instantaneous. Applying it requires patience, effort and training. The time it takes to reach your goal will be different for everyone. Yet, the recipe is simple. By mixing two essential ingredients, thought, and action, along with a dash of gratitude and a pinch of appreciation, you can create the life that you want.*

My friend, if you could even for a moment begin to become aware of the immense, eternal power you truly possess to create the life you dream of, never again would you ever judge your life. Never again would you ever feel inadequate or doomed to constant, daily struggle. I would dare to suggest that it's actually impossible to hate your life once you realize you're the one controlling most of it. But when perspective does change and when awakening comes - when the illusion of separation is stripped away, leaving only the lens of limitlessness - suddenly, life becomes nothing more than an adventure. In my own life, all those years ago, what I came to understand is that it's actually quite fun to create. It's fun to wake up every morning and create the life I desire. You see, I don't write books because I have to; I write books because I can. I don't travel the world teaching and helping to awaken others because it's my job; I do it because it's my joy. It's time to bring the joy back into your journey, my friend. It's time to become more thankful for all the opportunities that exist for you. Right now, even as you read these words, not even the sky is the limit on where you can go, what you can accomplish, and what you can create. There truly are no limits at all. In fact, there never have been.

Something truly remarkable begins to happen the very instant you begin to mix gratitude and thankfulness with your actions and your thoughts. Suddenly, not only does the entire world become yours for the taking and for the experiencing, but the entire journey begins to feel so much better than it did before. Whether you've ever taken the time to recognize it or not, you truly have so much to be thankful for. You've come so very far. You've already created so very much. Even those messy moments in the past were confirmation of just how truly powerful you are. You created those moments

ABOUT THE AUTHOR

Dr. Jeremy Lopez is Founder and President of Identity Network and Now Is Your Moment. Identity Network is one of the world's leading prophetic resource sites, offering books, teachings, and courses to a global audience. For more than thirty years, Dr. Lopez has been considered a pioneering voice within the field of the prophetic arts and his proven strategies for success coaching are now being implemented by various training groups and faith groups throughout the world. Dr. Lopez is the author of more than forty books, including his international bestselling books *The Universe is at Your Command* and *Creating with Your Thoughts*. Throughout his career, he has spoken prophetically into the lives of heads of business as well as heads of state. He has ministered to Governor Bob Riley of the State of Alabama, Prime Minister Benjamin Netanyahu, and Shimon Peres. Dr. Lopez continues to be a highly-sought conference teacher and host, speaking on the topics of human potential and spirituality.

Printed in Great Britain
by Amazon